10700217

American Dreamers

Other Books by Kelly Bulkeley

The Wilderness of Dreams:
Exploring the Religious Meanings of
Dreams in Modern Western Culture

Spiritual Dreaming:
A Cross-Cultural and Historical Journey

Among All These Dreamers:
Essays on Dreaming and Modern Society

An Introduction to the Psychology of Dreaming

Dreamcatching:
Every Parent's Guide to Understanding and Exploring
Children's Dreams and Nightmares (with Alan Siegel)

Visions of the Night:
Dreams, Religion, and Psychology

Transforming Dreams:
Learning Spiritual Lessons from
the Dreams You Never Forget

Dreams:
A Reader on the Religious, Cultural, and
Psychological Dimensions of Dreaming

Dreams of Healing:
Transforming Nightmares into Visions of Hope

The Wondering Brain:
Thinking about Religion With and
Beyond Cognitive Neuroscience

Soul, Psyche, Brain:
New Directions in the Study of Religion
and Brain-Mind Science

Dreaming Beyond Death:
A Guide to Pre-Death Dreams and
Visions (with Patricia Bulkley)

Dreaming in the World's Religions:
A Comparative History

American Dreamers

What Dreams Tell Us about the Political Psychology of Conservatives, Liberals, and Everyone Else

Kelly Bulkeley

Beacon Press
Boston

Beacon Press
25 Beacon Street
Boston, Massachusetts 02108-2892
www.beacon.org

Beacon Press books
are published under the auspices of
the Unitarian Universalist Association of Congregations.

© 2008 by Kelly Bulkeley
All rights reserved
Printed in the United States of America

11 10 09 08   8 7 6 5 4 3 2 1

This book is printed on acid-free paper that meets the uncoated paper
ANSI/NISO specifications for permanence as revised in 1992.

Text design and composition by Yvonne Tsang
at Wilsted and Taylor Publishing Services

Library of Congress Cataloging-in-Publication Data

Bulkeley, Kelly
  American dreamers : what dreams tell us about the political psychology of
conservatives, liberals, and everyone else / Kelly Bulkeley.
      p. cm.
  Includes bibliographical references and index.
  ISBN 978-0-8070-7734-4 (alk. paper)
  1. Political psychology. 2. Politicians—United States—Psychology. 3. United States—
Politics and government—2001—Psychological aspects. 4. Dreams. I. Title.

JA74.5.B85 2007
320.97301'9—dc22   2007045476

For my parents

Democratic nations scarcely concern
themselves with the past but readily
dream of the future; in this direction,
their unbounded imaginations
spread and grow without limits.

ALEXIS DE TOCQUEVILLE
Democracy in America

Contents

Introduction

The American Dream. It's a phrase that conjures up lofty visions of the nation's highest ideals and most noble aspirations (or, perhaps, memories of tedious high school English essays on *The Great Gatsby* or *Death of a Salesman*). Widely used in political speech, media commentary, commercial advertising, literature, art, and ordinary conversation, it's a shorthand way of referring to our country's core values, to those principles of enduring importance that define America's national identity. What's most striking when you first consider the various examples of politicians using this phrase is the basic agreement across the ideological spectrum about its essential meaning. Try the following test. Read the seven quotations below, and see if you can match them to the seven political leaders who spoke them.

1. The American Dream does not come to those who fall asleep... We have endured a long night of the American spirit. But as our eyes catch the dimness of the first rays of dawn, let us not curse the remaining dark. Let us gather the light.

2. [T]he substance of that dream...is found in those majestic words of the Declaration of Independence, words lifted to cosmic proportions: "We hold these truths to be self-evident, that all men are created equal, that they are endowed by God, Creator, with certain inalienable Rights, that among these are Life, Liberty, and the pursuit of Happiness." This is a dream. It's a great dream...God grant that America will be true to her dream.

3. Deep down, this country wasn't built on fear. This country was built on hope. This country was built on a belief in limitless possibilities, on a belief in dreaming big dreams.

4. For [more than two hundred] years, Americans have been united by a simple, common dream that tomorrow will be better than today. The promise of American life, handed on through a dozen generations, rests on this basic bargain: All of us should have the opportunity to live up to our God-given potential, and the responsibility to make the most of it...To remain strong in the world, the American Dream must be strong and alive here at home. And as we continue to navigate through these changing economic times, restoring the promise of the American Dream is the central economic issue of our time.

5. We believe in the American dream, because we've had a chance to live it. The American dream isn't about the accumulation of material things. It is much deeper and more profound than that. The essence of the American dream is the understanding that we are here on this earth and in this land for a higher purpose: to discover—and develop to the fullest—our God-given potential. Anything that stands in the way of the dream, we must fight. Anything that enhances the dream, we must support.

6. I have faith that with God's help we as a nation will move

forward together as one nation, indivisible. And together we will create an America that is open, so every citizen has access to the American dream; an America that is educated, so every child has the keys to realize that dream; and an America that is united in our diversity and our shared American values that are larger than race or party.

7. It's time to stop playing on people's fears and to begin asking what we can do together to make things better. None of us can afford to play politics as usual. We love this land of ours, because it's a special place where people are free to work, to save, to believe, to build a better future. The cynics may call it corny, but this way of life we all cherish is best summed up in three simple words: the American dream. From our beginnings as a nation, that dream has been a living, breathing reality for millions. It still is. But it faces serious threats.

A. President Richard M. Nixon, "First Inaugural Address," January 20, 1969.

B. President Ronald Reagan, "Remarks about the Congressional Elections," television broadcast, October 26, 1982.

C. The Reverend Doctor Martin Luther King Jr., "The American Dream," sermon delivered at Ebenezer Baptist Church, Atlanta, Georgia, July 4, 1965.

D. Senator Hillary Rodham Clinton, introducing the Democratic Leadership Council's report, "Saving the American Dream," July 19, 2006.

E. Governor and President-elect George W. Bush, speaking to the Texas legislature, December 13, 2000.

F. Senator Barack Obama, speaking at a Democratic rally in Tempe, Arizona, October 23, 2006.

G. Steve Forbes, *A New Birth of Freedom: A Vision for America* (Washington, DC: Regnery, 1999), 5.

Key: A-1, B-7, C-2, D-4, E-6, F-3, G-5

If you got most or all of them correct, congratulations! You are possessed of extremely sharp political intuition (or you're a very lucky guesser). If you got at least a couple right, you probably recognized the distinctive words and turns of phrase associated with major historical figures like Martin Luther King Jr. and Ronald Reagan. If you got none right, well, sorry. No more quizzes for the rest of the book, I promise.

Each of the seven quotes comes from a specific historical moment and political context, yet each of the speakers is seeking to evoke a timeless principle of national unity. In Martin Luther King Jr.'s Fourth of July sermon of 1965 he told his home congregation in Atlanta that the "substance" of the American Dream is rooted squarely in its founding document, the Declaration of Independence. Having just a few months earlier endured the racist violence accompanying the civil rights marches from Selma to Montgomery, King could easily have denounced the failures of the American Dream, but instead he praised the radically uplifting promise this "cosmic" principle offers to all people—"it is marvelous and great that we do have a dream, that we have a nation with a dream; and to forever challenge us; to forever give us a sense of urgency."

A few years later, newly elected president Richard Nixon gave the phrase a muscular conservative push toward daylight and wakefulness, with a poetic slam of sixties liberalism ("a long night of the American spirit") that still appealed to the core American ideals of hope and optimism ("Let us gather the light."). The irony, of course, is that five years later Gerald Ford brought a close to Nixon's scandal-ridden presidency when he proclaimed, "My fellow Americans, our long national nightmare is over."

President Ronald Reagan, vainly trying to fend off Democratic gains in the 1982 midterm elections (the Democrats ended up gaining twenty-six seats in the House of Representatives), spoke via a paid political advertisement to soothe the fears of a recession-plagued nation and remind people of their common belief in the American Dream's vision of freedom and prosperity for all, even while he acknowledged that the country was facing "serious threats" (mostly caused, he argued, by liberals who "spend and spend, tax and tax").

A similarly ambivalent tone appears in the passage from Steve Forbes's book, published in the midst of his quest for the 2000 Republican presidential nomination. As a wealthy businessman and libertarian, Forbes campaigned aggressively against taxes and government intrusion into the economy. But in the early pages of his book he appealed to the American Dream as a way of speaking about values beyond "material things," values that prize creative freedom above all else. Forbes felt confident he could readily distinguish those who support the dream from those who threaten it, and he seemed to be itching for a fight with the latter.

The man who won that year's Republican nomination, George W. Bush, went on to win the 2000 presidential election, but only after weeks of unprecedented national confusion, excruciating legal challenges, and bitterly contested recounts. Bush spoke to the Texas legislature the day after the U.S. Supreme Court decided the election in his favor, and his reference to the American Dream was aimed at reuniting a badly divided populace.

We know how well that's turned out.

Hillary Rodham Clinton's Democratic Leadership Council report served as a foundational statement of her priorities as she campaigned for the 2008 Democratic presidential nomination, and for her (as for Forbes, her ideological opposite) the American Dream expresses a belief that our country is, and has always been, dedicated to the freedom of everyone to develop his or her "God-given potential." The glorious promise of that dream is threatened, however, by the rising economic stress and anxiety felt by many Americans today, and Clinton has aimed her progressive policy agenda at relieving those domestic problems and restoring people's sense of financial optimism.

Her top rival for the nomination, Barack Obama, rose to political prominence not by business success or lengthy governmental service but by intelligence, charisma, and the inspirational power of his personal story (as narrated in his first book, *Dreams from My Father*). His campaign has benefited from the belief that supporting a mixed-race newcomer with a funny name for president is itself a way of promoting and actualizing the American Dream—if someone like Obama could be elected, maybe America really *is* a land of equal opportunity for all. When Obama counsels his followers to banish fear and embrace hope, he is simultaneously evoking the deepest American values *and* advancing his own political fortunes. (Much the same can be said of Hillary Clinton's efforts to become the first woman president.)

The difficulty of connecting these quotes to their speakers is no insult to anyone's intelligence or knowledge of current affairs. Rather, it shows the broad consensus among conservatives and liberals about what the American Dream means. This is where a new exploration of the political psychology of present-day America can begin. The ideals of freedom and equal opportunity, the virtues of daring and ingenuity, the indomitable hope for a better life in the future, the sheer joy in one's creative power and potential—when people speak of the American Dream they are evoking these time-honored principles of national identity.

This book takes the analysis of the American Dream one step further, into the study of actual dreams. How does the metaphorical American Dream relate to the literal dreams of Americans when they sleep each night? How much are people's private dream experiences influenced by the collective dreams of politics, religion, and popular culture? What do the themes and patterns of people's dreams tell us about their deepest political values? What are the conditions that enhance or diminish the quality of an individual's ability to dream and to participate in the American Dream? Exploring these questions will lead to fresh thinking about that sacred phrase of national character. Instead of invoking "the American Dream" as a piece of received wisdom about the desires and character of Americans, we will ground our discussion in the actual dreams of real people living in the contemporary United States. I'll present evidence showing that the playful fancies of people's dreaming imaginations can be interpreted as insightful expressions of the hopes and values that shape their lives. Dreams reveal not only our darkest instinctual desires but also our brightest spiritual ideals and most noble ethical virtues. If we want to learn something new about the American Dream in people's lives today, I propose we take a good, close look at how well the American people are sleeping and dreaming at night.

Yes, I admit this is an odd project. You might say *very* odd. Preposterous, even. That's OK. I understand the reaction. I've heard some variation of the question "What can dreams *possibly* have to do with politics?" countless times over the years I've been researching the subject (starting in 1992), and this book constitutes my best effort at an answer. In the pages to come I'll try to persuade you that people's sleep and dream experiences provide surprisingly accurate insights into the psychological underpinnings of their political beliefs and attitudes, whether they're conservative, liberal, or some combination of the two (as most of us are). The twenty-first-century study of dreams has moved beyond the psychoanalytic theories of Sigmund Freud and Carl Jung to encompass a variety of new empirical methods that can reliably identify connections between patterns of dream content and a person's most important thoughts, concerns, and preoccupations in waking life. By studying the images and emotions in people's dreams we discover a window into their deepest beliefs, darkest fears, and most inspiring ideals.

The core of *American Dreamers* is an analysis of the dream journals of ten "ordinary" Americans—that is, ten people from different backgrounds and parts of the country who volunteered to participate in a yearlong study of their sleep and dream lives. These ten Americans constitute a kind of long-term dreamers' focus group, and the coming chapters will explore the interplay between their dreaming experiences and their waking-life attitudes toward a variety of politically charged subjects.[1] To frame that analysis, I'll begin by outlining the statistical results of survey research on dreaming and politics, including an opinion poll (conducted on my behalf by the polling firm Greenberg Quinlan Rosner Research) of seven hundred demographically representative Americans who were asked several questions about their sleep and dream experiences.

The information from the dream journals is deep but narrow. The findings of the surveys are broad but shallow. We'll get the best picture of where the real psychological connections lie by putting these different methods together and seeing what patterns emerge most clearly.

Needless to say, there has never been a study like this before. I don't expect anyone to accept at first sight my premise that dream research provides meaningful insights into politics. But if you're willing to follow the evidence where it leads (evidence not only from my research but from many other scientific studies on sleep, dreaming, and political psychology), I guarantee you'll reach the end of this book with a deeper understanding of the unconscious dynamics of political ideals and partisan conflicts in present-day America.

Let me introduce the members of the dreamers' focus group.

Elizabeth is a fifty-eight-year-old hospital technician from Kentucky who has overcome the challenges posed by two divorces, several alcoholic family members, breast cancer and chemotherapy, and a number of other serious medical conditions requiring surgery. She considers herself a "survivor." For many years she has been energetically involved in the activities of her local Disciples of Christ church community. Elizabeth's a registered Democrat who says she's very liberal in her political beliefs, although she favors more freedom for gun owners and voted for George W. Bush in 2004.

Kip is a fifty-two-year-old ranch manager and horse trainer from northern California. Twenty years ago she took her seventeen-month-old baby and left her second husband to form a new family with her partner, Janet, a local sheriff. They've been together ever since, and Kip's daughter just graduated from college. Raised in a strict Catholic family, Kip is now very independent spiritually and laughingly considers herself a member of the "Church of the Living Hoof." She's a Democratic voter who detests President Bush, although in general she's not much interested in partisan politics. Her views used to be more liberal, but today she says she's "hardened up a bit," and if anything considers herself a political moderate.

Two married couples are included in the group of ten participants. The first of these couples went through an incredibly harrowing series of life challenges during the year of their journal keeping. Dan is a thirty-six-year-old Army Special Forces sergeant, a career soldier approaching the twenty-year retirement mark. He left for his third tour in Iraq during the journal-keeping year. Raised Catholic, he is politically conservative and believes the United States is engaged in a difficult but necessary long-term battle to "plant the seeds of democracy" in the Arab world.

Dan has been married for five years to Sophia, a thirty-one-year-old who takes care of their preschool daughter in their home on the outskirts of Dan's current base in North Carolina.

Sophia has always been an active dreamer, and in her local community she's known as someone who's available to talk about dreams. She's politically conservative and supportive of President Bush, but spiritually progressive in avoiding fundamentalist churchgoers and seeking alternative, non-Christian sources of wisdom. Soon after she began keeping her sleep and dream journal, and right after Dan received his latest deployment notice, Sophia discovered she was pregnant. Her journal thus became a record of her sleep and dream experiences across the nine-month term of her pregnancy, the last half of which she spent alone while Dan fought in Iraq.

The remaining six members of this group are, or have been, residents of the same rural, economically depressed county in western New York. Richard, a forty-eight-year-old hospital security manager, was born in Germany and emigrated with his family to the United States when he was one year old. His views tend to be conservative both religiously and politically (he's pro-Bush and pro–Iraq war). He used to be registered as a Democrat but recently changed his affiliation to Republican. Richard has a black belt in karate and is the founder of a successful, all-volunteer animal rehabilitation clinic in his community.

Grace, a forty-six-year-old preschool teacher, is Richard's wife. She says she's becoming increasingly conservative in her politics, and for the most part she supports President Bush, although she usually tries to pay as little attention to political current events as possible. Raised as a Catholic, she is now more interested in Christian spirituality outside of formal church settings. She and Richard have a nine-year-old daughter whom they adopted as a baby, and whose well-being is the core concern of their lives.

Will is a twenty-six-year-old man who grew up in a town close to where Richard and Grace live. He's well educated, highly intelligent, and knowledgeable about a wide variety of subjects. He's had difficulty in school and work, though, due in part to a hand deformity and a history of emotional troubles. Will is politically liberal and an avowed atheist—two qualities that further alienate him from the traditionalist mores of his conservative Catholic surroundings.

Paul is an eighty-year-old former Catholic priest who left his Franciscan order to marry an ex-nun. They raised four children, then divorced; he remains on good terms with her. Paul considers himself wiser now about religion than when he was a priest, and he leads a physically and socially active life. A pro-Bush, pro-war Democrat, he is an avid viewer of Fox Television news.

Lola is a forty-nine-year-old administrator at a retirement home. Her life was scarred by a heartrending tragedy ten years ago—in the heat of a family argument, one of her sons shot and killed her other son. They were fourteen and eleven years old at the time. The echoes of that awful fratricide continue to reverberate in her family, in her local community, and in her dreams. Lola was raised Lutheran, though she does not currently attend church. She prays regularly and considers spirituality to be immensely important in her life. Politically she's a conservative Republican, though she's sickened by the war (one of her nephews is in the army, serving his first tour in Iraq), and she can't bear to watch or listen to the news anymore.

Nadine is a twenty-four-year-old waitress living in Florida, engaged to be married and planning to move soon to Colorado. Raised as a Catholic in the same western New York region, Nadine recently moved away from home to start a new life on her own. She hasn't entirely rejected Catholicism, but she avoids organized religion in general, preferring to pursue her interests in Native American spiritual traditions. Her political views are mostly liberal (she worked for two years in Americorps, the youth volunteer program founded by Bill Clinton), although she is very upset that affirmative action policies limit the financial opportunities for "nonminority" people like her.

Without question, the lives of ten people can never be a perfect mirror of a nation of 300 million. Any research project that's based on data from journals, interviews, and surveys runs the danger of overgeneralization. Although I tried to cast as wide a recruiting net as possible, these ten dream-journaling volunteers included no Hispanics or African Americans, no one from the Midwest or Deep South, no high-income professionals, no evangelical Christians, no Jews or Muslims. Any claims made in this book must be qualified by those limitations.[2] Still, these ten particular people's lives embody so many of the challenges facing the country today that it's fair to view them as representing other Americans with similar experiences and convictions. We can't learn everything from this group, but we can learn a lot.

In the chapters to come I'll tell their waking and dreaming stories in relation to five politically charged issues in contemporary American society: the wars in Afghanistan and Iraq, the role of religion in private life and public policy, threats to the natural environment, people's struggles with work and financial security, and cultural issues involving sexuality, gender, and child rearing, collectively referred to under the heading "family values." Before that, I'll set the stage in chapter 1 by defining what I mean by the terms *liberal* and *conservative* and outlining what is currently known about the sleep and dream patterns of present-day Americans. The book will conclude with a reconsideration of the American Dream in light of what we've learned about dreaming and political imagination in the country today. Appendix 1 presents a set of politically related dream reports from other Americans in contemporary and historical contexts, and appendix 2 offers suggestions for further readings in the literature of dream research.

Introduction

The person usually credited with coining the exact phrase *the American Dream* is the historian James Truslow Adams, in his 1931 book *The Epic of America*. As the title suggests, Adams described America's rise to world prominence in terms of a grand narrative of world-historical significance. Although he did not whitewash the nightmarish suffering of the indigenous peoples or the African slaves whose lives were sacrificed for the benefit of the European colonists, Adams argued that America's historically unique character has been rooted in its visionary faith in the values of freedom, hope, and personal creativity. For him, the American Dream referred to the ultimate ideals that inspire both the nation and the life of each citizen. America's spectacular success derived, he said, from the ability of unprecedented numbers of people to imagine and pursue their own freely chosen goals. Adams identified a close, dynamic bond between national idealism and individual creativity, and in the pages to come I hope to shed new light on how that ideal is (and is not) being lived in the real-world experiences of contemporary Americans. I'll close here with Adams's most eloquent expression of its meaning:

> "The *American dream,* that dream of a land in which life should be better and richer and fuller for every man, with opportunity for each according to his ability or achievement. It is a difficult dream for the European upper classes to interpret adequately, and too many of ourselves have grown weary and mistrustful of it. It is not a dream of motor cars and high wages merely, but a dream of a social order in which each man and each woman shall be able to attain to the fullest stature of which they are innately capable, and be recognized by others for what they are, regardless of the fortuitous circumstances of birth or position ...the American dream that has lured tens of millions of all nations to our shores in the past century has not been a

dream of merely material plenty, though that has doubtless counted heavily. It has been much more than that. It has been a dream of being able to grow to the fullest development as man and woman, unhampered by the barriers which had slowly been erected in older civilizations, unrepressed by social orders which had developed for the benefit of classes rather than for the simple human being of any and every class."[3]

1

Conservatives and Liberals, Awake and Asleep

Let's start with an analysis of the two main political terms used in this book, *conservative* and *liberal*. Where did they originate? More important, what have they turned into?

In their common usage as adjectives, the words conservative and liberal carry meanings that are more or less opposed to each other. To be conservative means to safeguard something of value, to protect it for the future, to preserve its integrity against dangerous change. To be liberal means to act with generosity, tolerance, and openness toward others. Both terms come from Latin roots: *servare,* "to watch, keep safe," and *conservare,* "to keep, preserve"; *liber,* "free," and *liberalis,* "pertaining to a free man" (i.e., not a slave).[1]

The two words are used in nonpolitical situations every day (e.g., "a conservative estimate," "a liberal serving"), and there's no big mystery about their meanings. The difficulty comes in trying to fathom the alchemical processes by which their political connotations have shifted and morphed over time. At first sight, the political application of the terms would seem clear. Conservatives are cautious defenders of the status quo and liberals are freethinking agents of progress. Conservatism as a political ideology is usually associated with Edmund Burke's anxious writings in the late 1700s about the French Revolution and its violent attempt to create a new and better form of society. From Burke onward, conservatives have been people who question the wisdom of grandiose plans for social engineering and who prefer to maintain the traditional, trustworthy ways of living that have developed gradually through history.

The political ideology of liberalism first emerged in the Enlightenment philosophies of John Locke and Jean-Jacques Rousseau, whose writings played a central role in the fight to break free of the Catholic Church's monopoly on political power in early modern Europe. Since then, liberals have acted as champions of individual liberty in all spheres of life, envisioning a future of greater happiness and prosperity for everyone, a future that can be achieved by rational thought, cooperative effort, and scientifically designed technologies.

Liberals, generally speaking, fear the stifling oppression of religious dogma and affirm the natural dignity and power of human reason. Conservatives, meanwhile, worry about radical, uncontrollable change and desire stability and tradition above all else.

That's how it used to be, anyway. In twenty-first-century American politics the two terms have taken on rather different connotations. Conservatives today still advocate the classic values of social order, moral discipline, and religious faith. But most of them are also dedicated to the cause of free market capitalism, an economic system that is relentlessly destabilizing in its impact on communities and individuals (just ask anyone who's working two jobs or has seen his or her position moved overseas). Along with that, American conservatives stand out in their opposition to any real efforts to protect the natural environment—a strange position from an ideology supposedly devoted to preserving the heritage of the past from present and future dangers. And would anyone who values stability, traditional wisdom, and cautious skepticism toward grandiose plans for change ever have launched the current war in Iraq? Yet American conservatives did just that, and they continue to be the war's most passionate advocates. We've come a long way from Edmund Burke.

As for liberals, they remain forceful proponents of greater freedom of expression in American life and more generous care for the poor and underprivileged. They question the authority of religion in the formulation of public policy, and they push for scientific rationality in solving the problems of society. But in practice many of their methods have led to an out-of-control rise of state power and governmental interference with people's lives, limiting individual freedoms in order to favor the interests of one group over another. We can be sure that Locke and Rousseau would have been astonished at the gargantuan size and dizzying bureaucratic complexity of the American government today. At a certain point the state apparatus of liberal governance expands to a degree at which it stops being an agent of change and turns into a self-perpetuating colossus whose inertial mass makes any real change almost impossible.

The reality is that both terms have flip-flopped in their application to various political issues over the course of American history. This is one of the many reasons why we must be careful in how we talk about conservatives and liberals in America today. Ultimately, I'm going to argue that everyone's political attitudes are a mixture of both liberal *and* conservative ideals, and therefore it's misleading to separate people into two absolutely distinct types of political personality. For now, though, let's start with the conventional meanings of the terms and see where they lead.

American conservatives and liberals are represented by the country's two largest political parties, the Republicans and Democrats, respectively. Although some Democrats consider themselves conservative and some Republicans self-identify as liberals, the basic connection between each party and its publicly stated ideology is fairly straightforward. In demographic terms, liberals are more likely to live on the West Coast or in the Northeast, particularly in big cities. Conservatives predominate in the South, the Plains, the Rocky Mountain states, and rural areas generally. Conservatives tend to be more religiously observant, liberals less so. Liberals overall have higher levels of education, conservatives higher levels of income. Recent polling data indicate that more teenagers and young adults are self-identifying as liberals, while a greater percentage of retired and elderly adults consider themselves conservatives.[2] A majority of liberals are women; a majority of conservatives are men.

Because of their aggressive influence on electoral campaigns (fund-raising, advertising, lobbying, facilitating voter turnout), conservative Republicans and liberal Democrats wield enormous power in America. Their noisy struggles for partisan primacy cause so many problems for the rest of us that it's hard to believe how completely we've abandoned the efforts of the Founding Fathers to control the evils of "factions" in politics. James Madison wrote in *Federalist Paper #10* (1787): "By a faction, I understand a number of citizens, whether amounting to a majority or a minority of the whole, who are united and actuated by some common impulse of passion, or of interest, adversed to the rights of other citizens, or to the permanent and aggregate interests of the community." In his Farewell Address at the conclusion of his second term as president (1796), George Washington warned against the selfish schemes of "a small but artful and enterprising minority of the community" that seeks control of the government for its own purposes, thereby violating the basic constitutional principle of rule by and for the people as a whole. The Founding Fathers knew that factions were a necessary evil in democratic society (Madison admitted, "Liberty is to faction what air is to fire"), but they designed the Constitution with the specific intention of distributing power so broadly that no single faction could ever gain complete control over the country. Unfortunately, America today is controlled by two factions locked in a death grip of mutual hostility and governmental paralysis, each one choking the other's attempts to address the nation's long-term problems.

As another election approaches, the challenge for Americans will be to evaluate conservative and liberal ideas without succumbing to the fruitless entanglements of factional conflict. Easier said than done, to be sure, but the process begins by understanding the psychological origins of people's political passions. The more we know about the deepest unconscious roots of people's hopes, fears, and ideals, the better we'll be able to craft practical and realistic responses to the difficulties ahead. The ten members of my dreamers' focus group described to me at length their perspectives on the "red state versus blue state" partisan warfare of the past few years, and as I discuss their waking and dreaming stories in the chapters to come I'll be focusing especially closely on what they can tell us about the possibility of a creative integration of conservative and liberal ideals.

Sleeping and Dreaming

Next, we should lay out a few basic facts about the nature of sleeping and dreaming.[3] Sleep is a biological necessity not only for humans but for all mammals, along with countless bird, reptile, and amphibian species. To judge by its preservation through millions of years of evolution and its widespread distribution throughout the animal kingdom, sleep seems to serve a vital function in the survival and healthy functioning of "higher" forms of life. Like food, water, or air, we need regular amounts of sleep to survive. Loss of sleep leads to a sharp decrease in mental clarity, physical coordination, and emotional balance.[4] No ethically responsible research has pushed the question to its limit, but the available evidence suggests that if you totally deprive someone of sleep for long enough, he or she will suffer a complete psychophysiological breakdown and ultimately die.

Exact statistics are hard to come by, but it seems likely that people today are sleeping less than humans ever have before. *Homo sapiens* evolved as diurnal creatures, awake in the day and asleep at night. The ability to control fire allowed humans to create light in the darkness, and that new development probably altered their waking-sleeping patterns to some extent. But as a sleep-disrupting force in human life, nothing compares to Thomas Edison's nineteenth-century invention of the electric light bulb. From that time forward Americans have increasingly banished the night by illuminating their homes, streets, and cities with round-the-clock electrified brilliance, to the point where virtually no one falls asleep anymore just because the sun has gone down. The more recent inventions of radio, television, movies, video games, and the Internet have also contributed to the poor sleep habits of contemporary Americans, the vast majority of whom now stay awake far into the night. Add to that the soaring consumption of sugar, coffee, energy drinks, amphetamines, and prescription wakefulness aids like modafinil (marketed as Provigil), along with the intensifying pressures of working and competing in a global economy where someone, somewhere is always awake, and the result is a population of hyperstimulated, chronically sleep-deprived people.

If dreams occur during sleep, and sleep is this disturbed, then it's likely the dreams themselves will be affected, and for the worse. This will be a factor in all the dream reports we consider later in the book. Like millions of Americans, most of the ten members of the focus group struggle with their sleep, experiencing painful variations in the amount and restfulness of their nightly slumber. These people's dreams reflect the waking versus sleeping battles of American life and the hidden and not-so-hidden wounds they suffer as a result.

A dream, as I define it, is an imagined world of sights, sounds, thoughts, feelings, and activities that you (either as a character in the dream or a disembodied observer of it) experience during sleep. Dreams have been reported in cultures all over the world throughout history, and it's fair to say that dreaming is a universal feature of human experience.[5] Recent findings in cognitive neuroscience show that dreams are complex and meaningfully structured expressions of automatic brain-mind processes during sleep.[6] When we go to sleep at night our minds don't just shut off, to be turned back on when we awaken. Rather, the mind remains active throughout the sleep cycle. Indeed, sometimes the electrical and chemical processes of the brain become so intensified they exceed the levels found when a person is awake. Dreaming is closely associated with the brain state known as rapid eye movement (REM) sleep, although dreams are frequently reported from non-REM stages as well.

The bottom line is that every one of us is dreaming all night long, whether or not we remember any of it when we wake up. The best evidence gathered so far makes at least this much clear: dreaming is an integral part of being human. It's a natural outgrowth of the way our brains work, reflecting unconscious psychological processes that have developed over millions of years of evolution. Dreaming is as natural as breathing and as steady and rhythmic as the beating of our hearts.

While most people assume dreams are filled with bizarre imagery and disjointed nonsense, current research shows that people's dreams are actually much more likely to portray realistic settings and familiar situations. Many dreams are wild and freakish, but if you look at large numbers of people's dreams over long periods of time, you'll find a surprising degree of continuity with their ordinary waking lives.[7] Most people usually dream of places they know, being engaged in familiar activities, in the company of people from their daily lives. For example, if you're married, you probably dream fairly often about your spouse. If you have a stressful job, your dreams likely include lots of problematic work settings and bothersome colleagues. If you're a lifelong baseball fan, your dreams probably include more baseball references than other people's dreams do. In fact, the continuity is so strong and reliable that if you have nothing but a series of dreams to look at, you can accurately predict a person's primary waking life activities, biggest emotional concerns, deepest spiritual convictions, and most important personal relationships. It's a simple formula: the frequency and intensity with which a person dreams of something indicate its importance in his or her waking life. This principle of dreaming-waking continuity will serve as a valuable tool of analysis throughout the book.

The number of dreams people remember varies dramatically from person to person and through different stages of the life cycle. As a broad estimate, most adults recall one or two dreams a week, although the memories may be fleeting and disappear soon after waking. Some people remember multiple dreams every night, while other people claim they never dream at all. Women tend to remember more dreams than men, and more nightmares, too. Nightmares are especially frequent among children and adolescents, and usually taper off in adulthood. Repetitive nightmares are one of the core symptoms of posttraumatic stress disorder (PTSD), something we'll discuss later on. Dream recall seems to diminish with advancing age, although it's unclear whether or not that's an inevitable consequence of aging.

The difficulty in remembering dreams may stem from the dramatic changes in the brain that occur as we transition from sleeping to waking. When we awaken our brains are moving between two very different modes of neurochemical functioning and regional activation, and little of what we experience in the one mode is preserved in the transition into the other. Freud said we forget most of our dreams because our conscious minds don't want to face our unconscious desires. That may be true in some cases, but it's more likely the result of failing to fit the round pegs of dream experience in the square holes of waking memory.

People's waking habits are also an important factor in low levels of recall. If you're like most people, you wake up each weekday morning to an alarm clock. Think about that for a moment —your first instant of waking consciousness is filled with *alarm*, with a loud, jarring noise that jolts you out of sleep at a fixed time, immediately catapulting you into the waking world regime of schedules, tasks, and obligations. Dream memories that might survive a more gradual passage from sleeping into waking are for the most part instantly extinguished by the monstrous little device we dutifully place on our bedside tables. The speed with which people awaken and get out of bed has a big impact on whether or not they remember any dreams, and for most Americans their morning routines are decidedly adverse to dream recall.

And yet, dream recall can be increased by nothing more than (1) better sleeping and waking habits; and (2) simply wanting to remember more dreams. Paul, the former Catholic priest, is a good example of this. When he started the year of journal keeping he said that he rarely remembered his dreams, which might be expected given that he's an eighty-year-old male. But to his great surprise Paul found once he started the journal that he was suddenly remembering several dreams every week. His experience tallies with research showing that people's dream recall rises when they are encouraged to take a greater waking interest in their dreams.[8]

I like to put it this way: the more attention you pay to your dreams, the more attention your dreams will pay to you.

Several general features of dream content have been identified that will be helpful in analyzing and evaluating the reports to come. As already mentioned, many dreams include characters known to the dreamer from waking life. Almost all dreams include at least one other character—social animals that we are, we're rarely alone in our dreams. Men's dreams tend to have more male than female characters; women usually dream equally of males and females. Animals appear frequently in children's dreams (and in the dreams of tribal peoples), but rarely in American adult dreams. Nonhuman creatures or supernatural beings are also very rare, as are metamorphoses of one character into another. Most dreams involve friendly and/or aggressive interactions between the characters. Sexual experiences occur much less often, though their emotional and physical impact can be intense when they do. Every now and then something good and magical will happen in a dream, but more often the dreamer is the victim of a variety of misfortunes (getting lost, forgetting something, accidents, etc.). All human emotions appear in dreams, from ecstatic happiness and heart-wrenching sadness to violent anger and paralyzing fear, although a number of dreams involve no emotions at all. Researchers debate this issue, but I think people's dreams usually tend toward the negative end of the emotional spectrum, with a greater frequency of fear, anger, and sadness than happiness and contentment. We'll pay close attention to this in discussing the dream reports to come, because there's good evidence to believe that emotions in dreams are important expressions of unconscious psychological realities. The killer robot chasing you in a nightmare may not be real, but the emotional response of heart-thumping panic *is* real, and worth considering in its relation to potential threats and similar feelings in the waking world.

Another way to approach the dream patterns of Americans is to look at reports of what I call prototypical dreams. Research conducted here and in other countries indicates that people in all human groups periodically experience a set of recurrent dream scenarios that includes flying, falling, being chased or attacked, encountering a deceased loved one, and having sex.[9] These dreaming prototypes seem to be innate programs of the human imagination, ready to be activated at various points throughout a person's life. Their occurrence and frequency can be used as a broad index of the dreaming capacities of individuals and groups. As we explore the dream journals of the focus group, we'll find each person has a distinctive pattern of prototypical dreaming that reveals key aspects of his or her value system in waking life.

The last point to mention in this overview of current dream research regards what Jung called "big dreams."[10] A small but highly memorable portion of dreams involves intensified imagery, overwhelming emotion, powerful kinesthetic sensations, and/or brilliant conceptual insights. Although rare, such dreams make a vivid impact on the waking mind, and people remember them clearly for years afterward. While the vast majority of dreams is lost to the haze of memory, these big dreams are so powerful they literally cannot be forgotten. You don't have to buy into Jung's theory of the collective unconscious to recognize that these potent experiences represent an extraordinarily energetic and creative activation of the dreaming imagination. Most of my career as a researcher has been devoted to studying such dreams as they emerge in religious and spiritual traditions, where they have historically served as sources of guidance, warning, and consolation. I've also gathered hundreds of present-day survey and interview reports in which people have described their most intense and impactful dream experiences. In studying and analyzing these data I've discovered that such dreams regularly have the effect of provoking and stimulating the waking consciousness of the individual, expanding his or her range of self-knowledge and awareness of the world.

25

Tell me a person's most memorable dreams, and I'll tell you something true about the deepest psychospiritual energies coursing through his or her life.

Initial Correlations

Now let's put the two sides of the equation together and look at what's known about the sleep and dream patterns of American liberals and conservatives.

The short answer is, we don't know much. Other than my own work, I know of only two other small studies on the subject.[11] This is very much terra incognita as far as dream research goes. I first got interested in the dreaming-politics connection during graduate school, when my dissertation research on religious and psychological approaches to dreaming prompted an intriguing side question: Do dreams express meanings related exclusively to the personal concerns of the individual, or do they also relate to the collective affairs of their communities? I wondered because Western psychologists since Freud have said *no,* dreams are entirely individualistic, ego-focused, and devoid of meaningful references to public affairs. Most of the world's religious and spiritual traditions, however, have said *yes,* some dreams do speak meaningfully about collective problems, crises, and conflicts, in addition to and beyond the personal sphere of meaning. This seemed like an important theoretical dispute that could be settled by a relatively easy empirical test. In 1992 I asked twelve adult volunteers to keep a dream journal from October 25 to November 8, the two weeks straddling that year's presidential election (an unusual three-way contest between incumbent president George H. W. Bush, Arkansas governor Bill Clinton, and billionaire businessman H. Ross Perot).[12] The volunteers did not know what I was looking for in terms of political references, but they knew I was interested in dreams, so their recall rates for the journal period were probably higher than usual. As it turned out, half the people reported at least one dream during that two-week period that related to the election, politics, and/or politicians. Of 113 total dreams reported in the 12 people's diaries, 10 of them included an explicit election theme. As small as this study was, it was enough to refute the strongest version of the Western psychological theory that people *never* dream of political or community affairs. Here were six people out of a group of twelve who, with no more prompting than a request to keep a dream journal during election time, reported several such dreams.

Encouraged by that finding, I studied the different types of dreams with politically related themes and characters that people reported in response to my inquiries. (Selections of that material will be presented in appendix 1.) Next I tried looking at the dreaming-politics relationship from a different direction, to see if people from opposing political ideologies experience different kinds of dreams (whether explicitly related to politics or not). In the late 1990s I gathered a set of most-recent-dream reports from a group of college students evenly divided between self-described liberals and conservatives (fourteen men and fourteen women of each ideology, fifty-six participants total).[13] Using a content analysis method to identify the basic patterns in the dreams, I found that the conservatives had more nightmares, more dreams in which they lacked personal power, and a greater frequency of mundane, "lifelike" dreams, while the liberals had fewer nightmares, more dreams in which they had personal power, and a greater frequency of good fortunes and bizarre elements. This seemed plausibly related to the political realities of the time (during the second term of Bill Clinton), when most liberals were feeling pretty good about the country and most conservatives were smoldering with resentment and dissatisfaction. The findings also made sense in connection to the virtues of each ideology. Liberals came across in their dreams as more imaginative, flexible in their thought, and open to unusual possi-

bilities, while conservatives appeared more grounded in the realities of their present life and more aware of threats in the world.

The same findings could also be interpreted in a critical light
as indicating the crazy delusions of liberals and/or the paranoid
myopia of conservatives. When I reported my work at a dream
studies conference in the summer of 2001, the factoid "Conservatives have more nightmares" became the object of brief but
merry sport among talk radio hosts and political commentators.
When Terry McAuliffe, the Democratic National Committee
chairman, was asked about it, he declared, "If George W. Bush
were the leader of my party, I'd have trouble sleeping at night,
too." Not to be outdone as a dream spinner, Kevin Sheridan of
the Republican National Committee replied, "What do you expect after eight years of William Jefferson Clinton?"[14]

The size of my study wasn't large enough to say anything like
that with real confidence. But I was intrigued by the evidence
supporting the idea that people's political views are reflected in
the form and content of their dreams. It struck me as a legitimate
extension of the continuity principle between waking and
dreaming and worth pursuing in more detail.

Following the bitterly disputed election of George W. Bush as
president in 2000 and the terrorist attacks of September 11, 2001,
America entered a new political era. Conservatives ruled the
land, and they led the charge into the "war on terror," while liberals were left on the governmental sidelines, frustrated and pow-
erless to stop policies that horrified them. Between 9/11 and the
reelection of President Bush in 2004, I gathered several hundred
surveys in which people described their experience of various
types of dreams along with answers to questions about their
political views. I separated out of these surveys those individuals
who strongly identified themselves as conservatives (100 total,
69 female and 31 male) or liberals (134 total, 101 female and 33
male), and I compared their answers on the sleep and dream

questions.[15] Overall, the findings showed a great deal of similarity between the two groups. Conservatives and liberals both averaged around seven hours of sleep a night, with moderate to good sleep quality, about one dream recalled each week, and one nightmare recalled every few months. Along with that, the two groups displayed an almost identical pattern of the relative proportion among the dream types I asked about in the survey. Nightmares and sexual dreams were reported the most frequently, dreams of paralysis and mystical experience somewhat less, and dreams of snakes the least.

According to these findings, liberals and conservatives could not be described as different species, at least when it came to sleep and dreaming. People of both political persuasions shared a common substrate of sleeping and dreaming. The sharp differences at the level of ideology did *not* correspond to categorical differences in their sleeping and dreaming experiences.

But digging deeper into the data, I found some intriguing differences. Conservatives, especially conservative men, reported sleeping more soundly, while liberals, especially liberal women, had more troubled sleep and a more active, agitated dream life. Conservative men slept a bit longer, with better-quality sleep; they recalled the fewest dreams but had the most lucid awareness within them. Liberal women had the worst-quality sleep, recalled the greatest number and variety of dreams, and reported the most dreams of homosexuality. This polarity between soundly sleeping but minimally dreaming conservative men and poorly sleeping but wildly dreaming liberal women seemed to crystallize something important about the relationship of the two ideologies in the early years of the twenty-first century: the one is pleased with current power arrangements and disinclined to wonder about alternative perspectives, the other is frightened by and angry at the status quo and desperate to find new possibilities.

Overall, the dream reports from the conservatives were much

more mundane than those from the liberals, which was consistent with my previous study. Liberals had more dreams with unusual, distorted, fantastic elements than the conservatives, whose
dreams were more likely to portray normal characters, settings,
and activities. This was not an absolute difference, but on the
whole, the liberals had a wider sphere of dream experience, with
less anchoring in ordinary reality and a greater range of imagined
possibility, than did the conservatives.

The liberals and conservatives in the 2001–2004 surveys reported a roughly equal proportion of bad dreams and nightmares,
unlike my earlier study, which found a higher frequency of
nightmares among the conservatives. Given the small size of both
studies, this could just be a random variation. It could also be due
to the very different political climates of the two studies. Compared to the way they were feeling in the late 1990s, liberals in
the early 2000s were more upset and troubled, while conservatives were enjoying an enhanced sense of power and control. Perhaps the rise in liberal nightmares and drop in conservative bad
dreams reflected that.

Sleeping and Dreaming by the Numbers

As an additional test of these initial findings about the dream
patterns of liberals and conservatives, I commissioned an opinion
poll by a professional research firm (Greenberg Quinlan Rosner)
in August of 2007. I wanted to know if a national poll using
the highest-quality methods of political opinion research would
confirm what I'd discovered in my smaller-scale studies. The poll
gathered responses from 705 American adults, who were con-
tacted at home by means of random-digit-dialing telephone calls.
These people were demographically representative of the U.S.
population in terms of age, gender, region, and political outlook.
The margin of error for the overall statistical findings was plus or
minus 3.7 percent, slightly higher for the smaller subgroups.[16] As

mainstream opinion polling goes, this one is still on the small side. But the results are encouraging, particularly when considered in connection with my previous studies. I'm hoping other opinion researchers will begin asking sleep and dream questions in future polls to continue the process of filling out our knowledge of the full range and potentiality of the human mind.

My poll started with a standard question about the performance of the president. The results, I'm told, are consistent with the dispiriting numbers from other opinion research on this topic.

Bush Approval

"Do you approve or disapprove of the way George Bush is handling his job as president?" (%)

Strongly approve	14
Somewhat approve	18
Somewhat disapprove	15
Strongly disapprove	45
Don't know	7
Total approve	33
Total disapprove	60

Next came two questions about sleep.

Sleep Time

"How many hours do you usually sleep each night?" (%)

Fewer than 6	13
6–8.9	82
9 or more	4

Insomnia Nights

"How many nights per week do you have insomnia or trouble sleeping?" (%)

0	60
1–2	19
3 or more	19
Don't know	2

Here, too, the results are mostly in line with research from other sources. Even though we have reason to believe people exaggerate the length and/or quality of their sleep, these statistics give us a good place to start in exploring the connections between sleep, dreaming, and political outlook.[17]

The poll next asked participants about their experiences with seven prototypical dreams. The widespread occurrence of these kinds of dreams has been well documented by other researchers, and my study provides new information on their frequency across the American population.

Prototypical Dreams

"Have you ever dreamed of any of the following things?"

	Yes (%)	No (%)	Don't know (%)
A person who's now dead appearing alive	38	59	2
Magically flying in the air	22	76	2
Being chased or attacked	44	53	3
Falling	49	48	3
Sexual experiences	42	53	5
Being in a situation exactly like your regular waking life	55	40	5
Being aware you're dreaming and able to control the dream	38	58	5

As with the results of the sleep questions, I suspect the number of yes answers here is lower than the actual incidence of each dreaming prototype. How many people have experienced these dreams earlier in life but no longer remember them? How many people remember certain dreams but don't want to talk about them in a surprise conversation with a telephone pollster? I'm sure there have been odder polls in the history of opinion research, but I wouldn't blame the respondents if they felt startled by my dream questions and somewhat guarded about answering them. For reasons we'll discuss later in the book, many Americans show a justified reluctance to discuss their dreams with other people, no matter how well protected their anonymity.

Keeping those qualifications in mind, the results show the following distribution pattern among the seven kinds of dream. People reported flying dreams the least often, which I find surprising given the prominence of this prototype in the cultural lore of dreaming. Most people are aware that magical flying can occur in dreams, but it appears that relatively few Americans actually remember having such dreams themselves. The most oft-reported dream was the "mundane" type, involving an exact simulation of some situation from current waking life. This finding agrees with the data we'll consider a little later from the dream journals showing how the pressures and concerns of daily existence tend to dominate people's dreaming imaginations. Of the remaining prototypes, each of them seems to occur frequently but not universally. In all, 14 percent of the respondents answered no to all seven dream questions; 3 percent answered yes to all of them.

The most intriguing result to me regarded the "lucid" dream question. Usually considered an esoteric phenomenon restricted to Buddhist meditators and new age wisdom peddlers, little is known about its actual occurrence among the general public. The figure of 38 percent "yes" respondents to this question (worded using a high standard for lucidity that combines conscious awareness and volitional control) strikes me as highly suggestive. If this poll provides anything like a representative view of the U.S. population, it appears that tens of millions of Americans have personally experienced a lucid dream and know what it feels like to develop an alternative form of consciousness within the sleep state. That's a remarkable expression of dreaming potential in our present-day population.

Now let's get to the fun part. What happens when the sleep and dream questions are correlated with the different political ideologies of the respondents? There are two ways of looking at this. In the first, I separated the pro-Bush respondents (somewhat or strongly approving of him) from the anti-Bush respondents (somewhat or strongly disapproving) and compared the frequency of their answers to the sleep and dream questions.

Bush Approval and Sleep Patterns

Sleep patterns		Approve of Bush (%)	Disapprove of Bush (%)
Duration	Fewer than 6 hours a night	10	15
	6–8.9 hours a night	84	80
	More than 9 hours a night	4	4
Insomnia	Never	64	55
	1–2 nights a week	17	21
	3 or more nights a week	14	23

The sleep questions yield results very much like the findings of my earlier studies. People who disapprove of President Bush are more likely to sleep shorter hours and less soundly than people who approve of President Bush. If you're happy with President Bush, you're probably sleeping pretty well at night. If you don't like Bush, you're more vulnerable to poor sleep. Of the respondents in the poll who reported the worst sleep (three or more nights per week of insomnia), a blistering 62 percent strongly disapproved of the president's handling of his job, and 72 percent disapproved overall. Bad sleep and harsh feelings toward Bush seem to go hand in hand.

Bush Approval and Dream Patterns

Dream type	Approve of Bush (%)	Disapprove of Bush (%)
A person who's now dead appearing alive	34	41
Magically flying in the air	22	23
Being chased or attacked	41	47
Falling	47	50
Sexual experiences	40	44
Being in a situation exactly like your regular waking life	58	54
Being aware you're dreaming and able to control the dream	36	41

The dream questions also provide evidence in line with previous research. People who disapprove of the president were more likely to answer yes to all the dream prototypes, with the one exception of mundane dreams. The differences aren't huge, but they're consistent with what I've found before.

They're also consistent with the second type of analysis, in which I separated the conservatives (38 percent of the total) from the liberals (22 percent) and compared their answers to the same questions.

Political Ideology and Sleep Patterns

Sleep patterns		Liberal (%)	Conservative (%)
Duration	Fewer than 6 hours a night	12	15
	6–8.9 hours a night	82	80
	More than 9 hours a night	7	4
Insomnia	Never	54	63
	1–2 nights a week	17	17
	3 or more nights a week	28	16

Looking at the sleep data from this angle, the liberals report slightly more total sleep time than the conservatives, but also a higher proportion of severe insomnia.

The answers to the dream questions show an even greater difference between the two political orientations than did the pro-Bush and anti–Bush comparison.

Political Ideology and Dream Patterns

Dream type	Liberal (%)	Conservative (%)
A person who's now dead appearing alive	48	35
Magically flying in the air	23	20
Being chased or attacked	48	40
Falling	54	47
Sexual experiences	47	38
Being in a situation exactly like your regular waking life	58	56
Being aware you're dreaming and able to control the dream	44	34

Liberals answered yes more often than conservatives did to every one of the dream questions, even the one about mundane dreams (although that was the closest difference). Let me emphasize that plenty of conservatives answered yes to these questions, and many liberals answered no; the distinctions here are not absolute. As we get into the dream journals in the next chapter we'll find the picture becomes much more fluid, with conservative and liberal tendencies interacting in each person's dreams in unexpected ways. But if we take into account all the evidence presented so far, it seems reasonable to conclude (or at least accept as a working hypothesis) that conservatives are more likely to sleep well and remember fewer dreams, and liberals tend to sleep worse and remember more dreams. Until someone comes up with better data pointing in a different direction, the basic contrast we've found—conservatives as good sleepers and minimal dreamers, liberals as troubled sleepers and expansive dreamers —provides an empirically grounded principle to guide us in exploring the political psychology of dreaming. The dream journals we'll discuss in the coming chapters bring these patterns to life in a way that goes beyond mere statistics to a richer, more complex understanding of people's political belief systems.

2

The War on Terror

There's only one place to start a survey of the current political landscape: we're a country at war. After more than two decades of relatively brief and limited military actions (Grenada 1983, Panama 1989, the Gulf War 1991, Yugoslavia 1999), America in the twenty-first century has been fighting a bloody and ever-expanding "war on terror" against adversaries in Afghanistan, Iraq, and many other parts of the world. The dreams people have experienced during this grim era cast new light on the psychological impact of religiously motivated violence and open-ended warfare.

9/11

The traumatizing psychological effects of the terrorist attacks of September 11, 2001, were felt not just in New York City, Washington, DC, and rural Pennsylvania but all across the country. Beyond the thousands of people killed or wounded, beyond the tens of thousands of survivors, eyewitnesses, and rescue workers, beyond the hundreds of thousands of grieving relatives and friends, there were millions and millions of ordinary Americans who intently followed the round-the-clock news coverage and became swept up in the collective emotional maelstrom of shock, horror, confusion, sadness, and anger. Even today, several years later, most people can still remember the surrealistically intense fearfulness that gripped the nation in the days and weeks following the attacks (an anxious atmosphere worsened by the still-unexplained anthrax mail attacks in October of 2001).

In a study of dream content before and after 9/11 with a group of sixteen experienced dream journalers, Ernest Hartmann and Robert Basile found that dream imagery became stronger and more vivid following 9/11.[1] For each of the sixteen people, Hartmann and Basile looked at the ten dreams immediately preceding the terrorist attack and the ten dreams immediately following it. The post-9/11 dreams showed a notable increase in emotional arousal and image intensity, which we would expect in light of the continuity hypothesis. Surprisingly, however, none of the dream reports included a replaying of the image that dominated the country's consciousness in the attack's immediate aftermath —that is, no planes crashing into tall buildings. The participants in Hartmann and Basile's study were people who had regularly recorded their dreams for many years and who would presumably be especially sensitive to the dreaming impact of a waking-world catastrophe. The emotional trauma of 9/11 does seem to have reverberated in their dreams in terms of emotionally laden imagery, just not in literal references to the details of the attacks themselves. This makes sense, I believe, if we regard dreaming as an active meaning-making process that contributes to waking awareness, rather than a passive mirror of daily experience. In the days after 9/11 everyone knew *what* had happened—the urgent questions were what it *meant,* where it came from, and what we were going to do about it. A rise in dreaming intensity would be a natural expression of the sleeping mind's heightened efforts to answer those questions.

A post-9/11 research project I did with Tracey Kahan found that the dream content of a group of college students did in fact show a discernible impact from the terrorist attacks, but not in ways that could be easily predicted. The school these students attended was three thousand miles from "ground zero," so they were quite far removed from the physical location of the attacks. However, a student from the college was a passenger on one of the four hijacked planes, so the whole school community felt a direct connection to someone who died on 9/11. Of the twenty-one students who allowed us to read the dream journals they kept for a psychology class in the fall of 2001, sixteen of them reported a dream with a reference to some aspect of the terrorist attacks and/or the military actions taken in their immediate aftermath (we called these "incorporation dreams," using a more inclusive approach than Hartmann and Basile[2]). Two of the students had six or more incorporation dreams, a frequency that correlated with the especially strong and negative emotional reactions these two students reported in their waking lives following 9/11. To our surprise, the one participant in our group who was a personal friend of the student on the hijacked plane had no incorporation dreams at all, though she did experience a high degree of fear and distress in her post-9/11 dreams. Also surprising was a time-lag effect in the appearance of incorporation dreams. We expected to find more such dreams early in the journals, closer to the time of the precipitating trauma. But in fact they were scattered throughout the three-month period of time covered in the journals.

Our study did not gather the personal information that would be necessary to interpret the dreams more deeply. But several of the dreams revealed post-9/11 feelings and emotions that required no special analysis to understand, as a few brief examples can illustrate. A young woman worried about her generation's darkening future in this report:

I had a dream that everyone in their twenties had to go to war. It was not just limited to males; all people in my age group had to immediately go off to war... I remember being very nervous about going, and I was scared to go off with a bunch of people I didn't know.

Another young woman readied herself for the possibility of future attacks, imagining a scenario that most Americans vividly rehearsed in their own minds in the days and weeks following 9/11:

I was a passenger on an airplane and I was prepared in the event that there were hijackers on the plane. I made sure I had an aisle seat so that if there were terrorists on the plane I would be able to attack them.

A young man foresaw dire political consequences for his liberal home state following 9/11:

Russia launched nuclear missiles on California. The strangest part of the dream was that George W. Bush ordered Russia to do it, citing that California had been uncooperative in the war against Osama bin Laden and that the U.S. would best be served if the state of California were eliminated.

A young woman envisioned a surrealistic political dialogue:

Osama bin Laden came to speak at our college. The strange thing was, in my dream Osama was a woman. She was invited to speak at our college, so that we could gain a little insight into what exactly the Taliban was, and why they hated Americans.

It would probably make bin Laden hate us more than ever to know we're dreaming of him as a woman, but in a bizarre way I think this dream truthfully indicates the depth of changes necessary on both sides. If bin Laden could overcome the hypermasculinity of the Taliban's warrior ethos, and if Americans could open their minds to a better understanding of his and his followers' motivations, we might move closer to a world where such brutal attacks and violent outbursts would be less likely to occur.

Examples like these show that the dreaming imagination is not restricted to private individual concerns, but is in fact sensitive to the social and political realities of the waking world. More than that, these examples show that at least a few dreams seem to be creatively responding to the problems of the dreamer's community, offering novel perspectives on collective troubles. Not everyone has such dreams, at least in their most literal and direct form. But they reflect a dimension of political meaning that is latent in everyone's dreaming experience.

Afghanistan and Iraq

Although the rates of clinically diagnosed PTSD in New York and elsewhere seem to have receded to pre-9/11 levels, there's no doubt that the terrorist attacks and the actions taken in their wake still dominate national politics, and they will continue to haunt America's collective memory for many years to come. Immediately following the attacks, the nation's attention was centered on rescuing possible survivors and protecting against additional attacks. A remarkable unity of spirit and purpose took hold during those chaotic weeks. People did whatever they could to help—volunteered their time, donated their money, paid extra attention to public security, comforted each other. The attacks were directly aimed at the most prominent physical symbols of U.S. power (the World Trade Center, the Pentagon, the White House), and this anti-American targeting had the paradoxical effect of rallying people to a more intense and enthusiastic feeling of patriotism than many had ever felt before. For a brief but deeply energizing period of time, Americans experienced an authentic sense of national community, born of terrible suffering yet generating countless individual acts of bravery and compassion.

While all this was going on, officials in the Bush administration were rapidly preparing for two military invasions, first in Afghanistan and then in Iraq. Nearly all Americans approved when, in December of 2001, U.S. armed forces attacked the Taliban regime in Afghanistan and seized control of that country. More debate and disagreement preceded the invasion of Iraq in March of 2003, but a sizable majority of Americans strongly supported the mission when it was first launched. They accepted President Bush's argument that invading Iraq was an appropriate response to the 9/11 attacks and a justified measure to prevent future threats. Almost all conservatives approved of the Iraq war, as did most independents and many liberals.

War Support, Then and Now

"Do you approve or disapprove of the way
Bush is handling the situation in Iraq?"

	Approve (%)	Disapprove (%)
May 15, 2006	32	66
November 2, 2005	36	64
April 18, 2004	45	54
April 30, 2003	75	22

Source: Washington Post/ABC News Poll, released May 16, 2006.

Some people, almost all of them liberals, opposed the Iraq war when it was being debated by the president and Congress in 2002 and early 2003. These people argued passionately against

the invasion, horrified by the aggressiveness of the Bush administration's response to 9/11. During this time I heard several dreams
and nightmares from antiwar liberals. The frightening imagery of
their dreams clearly reflected their waking-world feelings of frustration, helplessness, and despair. A young woman from North
Carolina dreamed a couple weeks before the invasion:

> I was watching the news and suddenly discovered we were
> bombing Iraq. I was so upset that we were bombing the
> poor Iraqis and I saw so many people dying. It was a very
> distressing dream, and it seemed very lifelike. When I
> woke up I was sure that we had started bombing, when we
> had not yet begun.

The young woman's dream wasn't prophetic—by that point
everyone knew the invasion was inevitable—but it accurately
anticipated her emotional reactions to what was coming in the
immediate future. You might think it's cruel for the dreaming
imagination to force a person to experience such painful emotions before the feared event has even happened. But such dreams
actually serve a valuable function. By vividly imagining a future
threat, these kinds of nightmares promote greater conscious
awareness, readiness, vigilance, and adaptability. The unconscious logic is simple: if you can dream about it, you're better
able to handle it in the waking world.

Let me underscore this idea, because it's a guiding principle
throughout the book. One of the most important reasons we
dream is to prepare ourselves mentally, emotionally, and physically for the challenges of daily life. The evidence for this function
comes from many sources.

1. Neuroscientists have identified the activation in REM
   dreaming of brain patterns associated with the cognitive

processes of orienting in space, perceiving threats, and readying oneself to fight, flee, or mate.[3] Although researchers debate the range and precision of this rehearsal function, the neuroscientific data show that REM dreaming consistently occurs in tandem with the arousal of instinctual behavior programs. According to J. Allan Hobson, for many years the head of the neurophysiology laboratory at Harvard, "the motor programs in the brain are never more active than during REM sleep, [helping] to prevent their decay from disuse, to rehearse for their future actions when called on during waking, and to embed themselves in a rich matrix of meaning."[4]

2. Clinicians and psychotherapists have long known about the way dreams anticipate major turning points in a person's life, simulating possible actions and reactions in the safety of dreaming and thereby helping the individual approach those situations in waking life with greater awareness and confidence.[5] Rosalind Cartwright and Lynne Lamberg put it like this: "Dreams review the experiences that give rise to strong feelings and match them to related images from the past. They enable us to revise our pictures of our present selves and to rehearse our responses to future challenges."[6]

3. Developmental psychologists have presented systematic analyses of dream content that show a high prevalence of nightmares about threatening animals, particularly among young children.[7] In the early ancestral environment of humankind, wild animals were in fact an immediate and tangible danger to each individual's survival. What Antti Revonsuo calls the "threat simulation theory" suggests that dreaming evolved as a means for the individual to simulate potential dangers in the external environment and practice possible responses to them.[8]

To return to the case of the antiwar liberals, then, their night-mares were threat simulations of what they accurately perceived to be imminent dangers in their present lives. Their frightening dreams served as a kind of psychological bracing against the wak-ing-world sorrows to come. A forty-one-year-old woman who worked as a technical writer at an insurance company in Alabama told me that two nights after the invasion began she had this dream:

> It started with bombs dropping and soon evolved into a sort of science fiction scenario with underground bunkers and force fields. These force fields could automatically rec-ognize friend from foe—that baffled me and, frankly, worried me that I would maybe not be able to get in. Above ground was like a sprawling housing project... Once you got into the underground you were safe: the force fields made you safe from the bombing that was going on overhead. They were trying out new kinds of bombs that were just flashes in the sky, like neutron bombs, I suppose, designed to kill but not to destroy the buildings.

This woman was strongly opposed to the war, an attitude that put her sharply at odds with her pro-war family, neighbors, and office colleagues. A few days after the dream she became involved in an angry e-mail exchange with coworkers at her company. Some of the employees were soliciting charitable donations for U.S. troops in Iraq, and she replied by suggesting that people also consider visiting an Oxfam Web site. Instantly she became a pariah in the office, scorned and rejected by everyone. The same attitude of "with us or against us" hostility she so disliked in the Bush administration's foreign policy she now found directly aimed at her in her work life. Several weeks after the initial exchange she told me, "I am still involved with discussions between me, my manager, and human resources. Basically, it's an extremely uncomfortable position to be in right now, and you can rest assured that absolutely no one has stopped by my desk to support my input." Much as her dream anticipated, this liberal American found herself in a dangerous situation of war-related conflict, where her identity as "friend" or "foe" was called into question and her best hope for survival was to move herself (and her minority political opinions) underground, safely out of sight.

My initial efforts to gather war-related dreams yielded very little from the people who supported the war. Given that most Americans belonged to the pro-war camp, this struck me as a significant shortcoming. I knew my primary sources of information (college students, members of dream-sharing groups, academic colleagues, Internet contacts) were mostly comprised of liberal people opposed to the war, but I didn't expect this would lead to such a dramatic difference in the dream reports. Perhaps, following the research results discussed in the previous chapter, liberals in general have more intense and disturbing dreams than do conservatives, and that's why I didn't hear as many reports from pro-war people. That seemed a plausible conclusion, but I couldn't really be sure of it without a more determined effort to investigate the dream lives not only of liberals but of conservatives as well. Most dream researchers, myself included, tend toward the liberal end of the political spectrum, and so do the psychology students and therapy clients who volunteer for our research projects. In order to correct for that, the dreamers' focus group I've gathered for this book has a decidedly conservative, pro-war political tilt. Eight of the ten people said they agreed with President Bush's decision to invade Iraq, a ratio that's roughly proportional to the percentage of Americans who initially supported the war. One of my biggest goals in writing this book was to expand the range of political perspectives represented in dream research and to see what new insights emerge from a more inclusive approach. If the study of dreams is really going to say something new about the political psychology of contemporary America, it has to devote more detailed analysis to the sleep and dream patterns of pro-war conservatives.

A Soldier's Dreams

To push that premise one step further, I wanted to include the voices not only of those who supported the Iraq invasion but those who have actually been fighting it. The war's emotional impact on the lives of America's soldiers and their families has been immeasurably more painful than it has been for the rest of us, and any discussion of the psychological consequences of post-9/11 life should take their experiences into account. That's why I was grateful that Dan and Sophia volunteered to be part of the journal-keeping group. Dan's unit has made three trips to Iraq, and Sophia has been doing everything she can to hold their young family together while he's gone. They have truly been on the frontlines of America's military response to 9/11, and their story offers a helpful perspective on the psychological dynamics of present-day American conservatism. I don't want to overideal-ize them—every individual has flaws and weaknesses, and Dan and Sophia are no exceptions. But I do believe they represent some of the most important virtues and character strengths asso-ciated with a conservative political outlook. These virtues and strengths express themselves very clearly in their dreams.

Dan's father was a career army soldier who fought two tours in Vietnam. His early childhood was spent in small towns near the bases where his father was stationed. When he was ten years old, Dan's parents got divorced. At first he lived with his father, then with his mother through the rest of his teenage years. Starting in sixth grade he took a job delivering newspapers, with a route that required him to get up at 4:30 a.m. most days of the week (earlier on Sundays because of the extra customers). He did this for five years, developing an ability to operate on minimal sleep that has served him well in later life. His most memorable dream, and worst nightmare, began when he was seven or eight years old. It was short but very intense, and it recurred several times a year throughout his teens:

> Someone was breaking into our home and had a laser knife. They were killing all my family members, slicing through their heads.

A gruesome image, very scary and impossible to stop. One time Dan went sleepwalking during the dream and woke up to find himself outside on the roof of the house, a bundle of clothes in his hands, trying to escape the knife-wielding murderer.

This is not unusual, as children's nightmares go. The fear of losing one's family is a natural anxiety in childhood. It reflects a young human's dawning awareness of the dangers he or she would face if such an attack were really to happen. Frightening dreams of wild animals and evil monsters occur to most children and adolescents, and strange bouts of sleepwalking occasionally accompany these haunting dreams. Almost everyone has nightmares of repeating themes or scenarios, and these recurrent elements usually indicate a primal fear in the person's waking life.[9] What's interesting about Dan's recurrent nightmares is that they continued until he was eighteen, and then stopped—when he enlisted in the army. It would be too strong to say that joining the army made his nightmares go away, but considering what Dan has done with his life (rising through the ranks to become a Special Forces sergeant highly trained in hostage rescue missions), it seems fair to say that his waking-world career has been an adaptive response to the anxieties appearing in his childhood nightmares.

When the attacks of 9/11 occurred, Dan and Sophia had been

married for only eight months. Sophia says she watched the television coverage that day with a sinking feeling, knowing it meant her husband would soon be activated for whatever U.S. counterattack was sure to be coming. For his part, Dan says his initial reaction was shock at the fanaticism of the 9/11 terrorists. He couldn't understand the strange passions that led them to commit acts of such extreme violence—"I can't fathom their idealism." He and his unit were quickly mobilized and sent overseas, and for the next six years they worked a four-months-away, four-months-back rotation. Dan's faith in the mission has remained strong throughout, and if anything it has grown beyond the original cause of post-9/11 self-defense to embrace a deeply American belief in the transformative goodness of democracy. He sees the Iraq war as part of a long-term effort that may not bear fruit for many years but that we must see through to the end. "Their government is slowly building; their security forces are slowly building. We are committed, whether right or wrong, and we're doing the right thing sticking to it." He's angry at media reporters who mischaracterize events in the war, and he's disappointed by fellow Americans who expect quick and easy results in a historic battle to bring democracy to a country "dead smack in the middle of the Arab world."

Before he began keeping the sleep and dream journal in the spring of 2006, I asked Dan (like all the other journal keepers) to fill out a brief introductory survey, which included a question about his "most recent dream." This is a standard dream research question, and I wanted to have that kind of basic information before the journal process got started. Dan answered with this:

Most recent dream was déjà vu experience during a mission in Iraq. We (our team) were moving along a street, and the way it was laid out and the people there reminded me of seeing it before, in a recent dream.

51

What people call déjà vu experiences are often exactly this, memories of dreams that flash into mind when triggered by something identical in waking life. Once again, this reflects the anticipatory power of the dreaming imagination and its connection to brain-mind functioning.[10] In REM sleep, when most but not all dreaming seems to occur, the limbic system of the brain becomes especially active, stimulating a heightened emotionality and instinctual responsiveness. The occipital lobe of the brain, which processes visual perception from the eyes, decreases its activity in REM sleep, but there's a corresponding rise in activation among the parts of the brain responsible for imagination, memory associations, and so-called secondary visual processing. Rational consciousness recedes in dreaming, and a different way of knowing emerges—a knowing that draws upon our tremendous mental powers of intuition, synthesis, and creative forethought. As I've already suggested, one of the most valuable outgrowths of these spontaneous mental activities are "threat simulations"— that is, visions of potentially dangerous situations we might face in the near future.

Military history certainly provides evidence to this effect. Vivid dreams coming to soldiers before battle have been reported in ancient India, China, Greece, and Rome. Islamic tradition has known of prebattle dreams ever since the Prophet Muhammad reported two martial dreams in sura 8 of the Qur'an. No less an American military hero than General George S. Patton was an active dreamer who regularly woke up in the middle of the night during World War II and called his personal secretary to come and write down the battle plans that had appeared in his dreams.[11] This shouldn't be seen as something weird or superstitious. It's simply a reflection of a basic ability of the human mind that enhances our waking-world vigilance and readiness for effective action. For a soldier about to enter combat, any extra degree of awareness and sensitivity to danger can provide a life-saving advantage.

The four months of Dan's journal covered the time leading up to what he knew would be his last tour in Iraq. He was nearing the twenty-year point in his career and planned to retire in 2007. In those spring months he slept long and well, averaging eight and a half hours a night. About a month before he left, when the training regime picked up, his sleep time diminished to about seven hours a night, though he still reported good sleep quality. This is something to take note of—the overall *non*troubled quality of Dan's sleep. As someone who has experienced a great deal of wartime violence, he would certainly be a candidate for post-traumatic stress disorder, and yet he sleeps well and suffers none of the standard symptoms of PTSD. I asked him about this, and he attributed it to a combination of things: long experience in the military, the comfort of being married to Sophia, and trust in the professionalism of his team members. It's not that he's insensitive to the horrors of war; it's just that he's blessed with a very strong support network, and he's developed a lifelong ability to sleep well despite adverse circumstances.

His journal included thirty-one dreams, for an average recall rate of about two dreams per week. The majority of his dreams portrayed realistic settings and familiar activities; only a few dreams could be classified as "bizarre" in terms of containing magical and/or unrealistic events. Most of his dream reports were fairly short (around seventy-five words), exhibiting few explicit emotions. The most common theme (in nineteen of the thirty-one dreams) was military activity, consistent with the primary concerns of his waking life. In many of these dreams he was struggling to do his job despite external obstacles and poor performance by his colleagues. The same high standards of professional skill that he followed in his waking life also guided his behavior in dreaming. He did experience a few nightmares, but they were not classic PTSD nightmares in the sense of vividly reenacting a particularly horrible event from waking life. A few had nothing to do with the war at all. For example:

> I had a dream that I was attacked by a snake. I was in a creek or river and saw a snake come after me. I couldn't get away from it. It was like a big one, an anaconda or something. I was up to my neck/chest in water—he came right up to my face. I tried to scare him away, breathing on him and yelling, "Yah, yah," but that only provoked him. He struck at my neck three or four times. I think I got my hands on him at one point after he struck me a couple times.

About a week earlier Dan had watched a TV show about man-eating snakes, so the images of the dream were probably triggered in part by that recent memory. But something more is going on in a dream like this, which activates a very ancient program in the dreaming mind. This basic nightmare scenario—being relentlessly attacked by a big, frightening creature—harkens straight back to the existential fears of childhood, fears that remain very much alive in the unconscious minds of adults, even battle-tested warriors like Dan. For someone raised Catholic, the encounter with a life-threatening snake takes on an extra degree of significance in relation to the biblical story of the evil serpent in Genesis. To dream of fighting against a snake is, in this sense, an apt metaphor for Dan's waking-life mission to fight the enemies who threaten our country's interests.

I've spent a lot of time emphasizing the continuities between dreaming and waking, but now I want to show why it's also important to pay attention to dreaming-waking *dis*continuities—to those aspects of dreams that are bizarre, impossible, fantastic, incongruous, and so on. We've seen that the dreaming mind has the ability to generate realistic, accurately detailed settings and activities from our ordinary daily lives. What, then, is happening when the dreaming mind creates an experience that deviates in some dramatic way from the norms of the waking world? Some researchers argue that these bizarre elements are meaningless because they are caused by random neural firings in the brain during sleep.[12] Other researchers have found evidence showing that bizarreness in dreaming may represent the enhanced powers of creativity in the sleeping brain.[13] The latter view is more consistent with my experience. I've found in many dreams it's precisely the most bizarre and unusual elements that express the most thought-provoking meanings. By looking for both continuities and discontinuities in dreams, we're able to discover both long-term patterns and creative flashes of insight. That, at any rate, is the approach I use when I consider a dream like this, which Dan experienced in late spring. It was actually two dreams in a single night, and he titled them together "War":

> I am in a postholocaust area, wrecked cars everywhere, total devastation. It's a survival of the fittest situation. It was horrible, I had to walk long distances to find food and water. There were decomposing bodies lying everywhere and you literally had to walk over them. It was a yucky dream—felt like the United States. I don't remember seeing anyone else except I was almost run over by a huge truck that collected trash. I didn't know what it was and had to jump out of the way.

He woke from this in the middle of the night feeling disturbed and agitated, and we can readily understand why. The bottom of Dan's world falls out in this apocalyptic nightmare. He's thrown into an alternative reality in which America has been consumed by death and destruction. Life as he knows it has ended, and everyone he's ever known or loved is gone. He's alone, reduced to scavenging for survival and dodging strange, menacing vehicles. Dan is not the first person ever to have such a horrible dream. Vivid nightmares involving utter desolation and the loss of all human contact are rare but very memorable when they do occur. They reflect what I call a "titanic" awareness of the ultimate existential power of entropy. (In Greek mythology, the Titans were the "Elder Gods," the primordial deities who were born of heaven [Ouranos] and earth [Gaia] and who, for untold ages, ruled over the cosmos.) Titanic dreams tend to be unusually abstract and disembodied, filled with tremendous force and power; the dreamer often appears alone in dark, empty settings devoid of organic life. These experiences reflect, I believe, an extraordinary depth of psychological awareness. We know in the very fibers of our being that all material reality is moving toward death and destruction. Most people don't dwell on such unhappy entropic thoughts, but every now and then a titanic nightmare will blast its way into consciousness as a reminder of this primordial truth of our lives as embodied beings.

Why would this be an important moment for Dan to pay attention to such a dark, painful insight? The answer comes in his second dream:

> I am an observer or advisor to a small military outpost. We get attacked by an air assault, planes dropped tons of soldiers all over our camp. It was men and women in our camp. I was with a small number of soldiers who escaped, we were walking through the swamp, doing good, when another group of escaping soldiers ran right into us— bringing the enemy on top of us. We all ran, and I found an empty refrigerator to hide in. I remember pulling some seal off the door so it wouldn't seal on me. I shut the door

and waited. The enemy found me, the guy was mad at me for some reason—I wouldn't tell him something or I lied—anyway, he wanted to cut off my finger. He asked if I was part of A11 (my company) and I said no. I noticed a soldier from our camp who was now an advisor or emissary for the enemy. He stood up for me and saved my finger, and my life.

Here Dan finds himself in a more realistic wartime setting, closer in its details to his recent and upcoming duties in Iraq. The attack, however, comes from a strangely unrealistic direction. Dan and other U.S. soldiers depend on control of the skies, yet his dream portrays a dangerous assault from above, and not in the form of bombs but rather of "tons of soldiers" dropping down upon them. The soldiers seem to be enemies, reflecting the vast numbers of hostile fighters in Iraq, but they also appear like U.S. reinforcements in their mode of arrival and their mixed-gender composition. The battle goes against his side; he and a few others escape, and then his lifelong military training takes over. The theme of professional competence that's so important to Dan appears again, as he and the others move through a "swamp"—not the first time that metaphor's been used to describe the current location of the U.S. effort in Iraq.

At this moment in the dream the greatest danger appears, and it's not from the insurgents. Rather, it's the lack of competence of other American forces. Another group of U.S. soldiers blunders into Dan's group, leading the enemy right to them. It's the tactical equivalent of a friendly-fire incident, something that's a real and constant concern of Dan's in Iraq. The odd appearance of a refrigerator signals the desperation of his plight; he's reduced to hiding in a cold box. The enemy captures him, and now he faces every soldier's worst nightmare: will he deny his unit to save himself? It's a crisis of loyalty that also resonates with the Christian story of Peter denying Jesus. The threat of cutting off his finger reflects the real danger of maiming for U.S. soldiers, and it echoes the psychoanalytic notion of castration anxiety, further intensifying the existential dimensions of the conflict. Salvation comes from an unexpected source, an ally who's working with the enemy. At his weakest moment, when everything seems lost, Dan is rescued by a friendly soldier who's able to negotiate with their foes. There's an element of reassurance in this dream—Dan can trust in forces beyond his own personal strength. There's also a quality of honest evaluation of what's going on in the war. His dreaming mind was imagining what it would be like to lose, to be defeated, to fall short of his ideals. He was about to leave home one last time to fight on behalf of his beliefs. In anticipation of that, he's dreaming of what most concerns him: not personally dying (if anyone could survive in a wartime or postholocaust setting, it would be him), but the possible failure of his mission.

One more of Dan's dreams is worth mentioning for its pointed relevance to the American effort in Iraq. It came about six weeks before his deployment, when his team was beginning to train, receive briefings, and gather equipment for its upcoming duties. He and the others had just been informed of a change in the type of body armor they would be issued. The quality of one's body armor is, understandably, a touchy subject for soldiers about to enter combat. Dan's unit was shocked and angered by the unexpected switch. The new body armor was cheaper and less protective than the old type, and word was going around that the change was due to political lobbying by the new type's manufacturer. During this tense time, Dan had a short but vivid dream:

> The commander was going crazy, he was trying to kill himself. We were all trying to stop him. We weren't in uniform, not at the company. I don't know where we were.

In fact the commander was even more outraged than the rest of the unit at the body armor situation. As their commanding officer, he was responsible for the well-being of his troops, and weaker body armor made them significantly more vulnerable. Dan's dream envisioned the commander being pushed so far that he loses all emotional self-control and essentially turns his thwarted anger upon himself. It wasn't a totally unreasonable fear under the circumstances, and Dan acts in the dream like he would in waking life: he tries to protect the commander from harming himself, fighting to keep the unit together. The other men in the group are not wearing their uniforms, perhaps because they're not soldiers doing their duty—they're just a small, tightly knit group of men struggling to help one of their own in a time of crisis. At a more personal level, the dream also hints at Dan's private struggle to master his own angry emotions and keep his focus on the success of the mission.

The Home Front

When Sophia married Dan in 2000, she knew what would be expected of her as the wife of a soldier. But no one knew how much life would change for all Americans, especially military personnel and their families, after the 9/11 attacks. Just a couple of weeks earlier, Sophia and Dan had happily discovered she was pregnant, and her first appointment with her obstetrician was scheduled for September 12. The day of the attacks, she says, as she watched the base rapidly shift to a total security lockdown, "I could not help worrying about my own husband and how our lives were going to change forever...I knew in my gut that Dan would be deployed and gone when my baby was born."

Sophia's ability to survive and maintain some degree of psychological health over the past several years has depended on personality strengths that also emerge in her dreams, although in ways almost completely the opposite of Dan's dreaming. By any measure, Sophia is a voluminous dreamer. She remembers at least one dream almost every night, and over the thirteen total months of her journal keeping she recorded 276 dreams. Of those reports, almost half were two hundred words or longer. Two-thirds of her dreams included at least one explicitly mentioned emotion. Compared to Dan she had far more bizarre dreams, with a wider variety of characters, settings, and activities. Her nightmare frequency showed a sadly understandable rise in the two months leading up to her husband's deployment, culminating in a "very distressing" dream two nights after he left:

> Long and horrible... Dreamt Dan was married to both my sister Brenda and myself. He was taking me to his place of work where we ended up going on a mission This workplace was under the guise of a normal office with lots of employees, doing normal work—but he was actually a spy or undercover operative doing dangerous missions, but like a contract worker. At one point I end up with him in a new helicopter vehicle that we have to jump out of. He has tons of hi-tech vehicles and equipment and acts ambivalent through the whole dream. I know that Brenda is expecting him to come home later to take her out, but the employees cook a huge feast and everyone sits to eat—but I am not invited to sit and I get extremely upset. It escalates through the dream. I plead and cry to him to take me home but he won't. The dream revolves around me wanting to go home but can't.

No special expertise is needed to appreciate the painful feelings expressed in this dream. At that particular moment Sophia had no idea exactly where Dan was and what he was experiencing. The news media were reporting a sudden outbreak of fighting between Israel and Hezbollah in Lebanon, which was inflaming regional tensions even further. Sophia's nightmare showed how desperately she wished her husband could come home to care for her and their young family. Yet she realized in the dream that she was helpless to stop him from joining the battle—another bitter but necessary truth from the dreaming imagination. Sophia said the dream actually reminded her that Dan was trusting in her strength to hold on until he returned. She felt the bizarre detail of Dan being married to both her and her sister Brenda showed that Dan was trying to bring a tough, self-controlled part of Sophia into the realm of his work (Brenda is a softer, more emotionally sensitive person). Sophia worried she wouldn't be able to keep herself together and do what needed to be done.

After this she almost never dreamed about the war or the military (though she did note in her journal—with multiple exclamation points—the day that Iraqi insurgent leader al-Zarqawi was found and killed). She did dream a lot about Dan, however. A couple of months after he left, she talked to him on the phone for an hour in the middle of the night, then went back to sleep and dreamed this:

Dan and I and Mandy [their daughter] bought this house somewhere close to the beach, along with a big houseboat. We were wealthy. There were people after us, Dan could leave to work on the boat and get kidnapped for days at a time. Each time I would worry—then he'd come back saying it was the Serbs or another terrorist group. His hair was scraggly and growing longer. We finally decided to escape—Dan was gone for a few minutes and this pack of dogs was sent to find us. Mandy was with me when we saw the dogs. They were huge, expensive hunting breeds. I screamed for Dan and grabbed Mandy to throw her in the house. We decided to try and escape on the boat. I don't know who was after us but they were Mafia types.

A happy fantasy of family togetherness and prosperity turns into another frightening instance of that universal nightmare scenario, a violent animal attack. For Dan, it was a snake; for Sophia, a pack of dogs, apparently sent by the "Mafia types" trying to kidnap Dan and force him into a different kind of "family" whose interests are hostile to his family Sophia and Mandy. What's surprising, really, is that Sophia didn't have *more* nightmares like this during Dan's deployment. In fact, most of her dreams during this time were not excessively negative or upsetting. She often faced dream situations of difficulty and frustration, but more often than not she managed to keep her own personal focus and intensity. As we'll see in more detail in the next chapter, many of Sophia's dreams involved feelings and images she considered to be spiritually meaningful. Although very different from Dan in many ways, Sophia shares this key virtue with him: a total determination to remain true to her ideals in the face of extreme adversity.

Fading Hopes

As I mentioned before, most of the people in the dream journaling group originally supported the invasion of Iraq. Richard, the hospital security manager, declared that he "100 percent agreed with the Iraq war," going so far as to say, "I would enlist if I were younger." However, even Richard has become fatalistic about the prospects for a successful outcome. He still approves of President Bush's firm, unwavering leadership, and he still believes America was defending its vital interests by invading Iraq, but he's no longer hoping for an easy end to the war: "All we can have is better security." Paul, the former priest, expressed similar feelings when he said, "I just hope we hang in there till we're not needed." Grace, the preschool teacher, and Lola, the retirement home administrator, both agreed with the invasion as a necessary response to 9/11, but they've become so distressed by the war's length and savagery that they deliberately avoid reading or hearing news about it. Grace says, "I support the effort now but I'm anxious to pull out." Lola says it's all too "overwhelming and depressing," especially when she thinks of all the other parents losing their children to violence on 9/11 and in the war. Lola has a twenty-one-year-old nephew who recently joined the army and was just sent on his first tour to Iraq, and she's afraid of another premature death among her family's children.

Although they're liberal Democrats in most other ways, Elizabeth the hospital technician and Kip the ranch manager initially supported the war and believed in the democratizing ideals behind the invasion. Their pro-war motivation came less from fear of terrorism and more from a hope for positive change in the Arab Muslim world. However, they're both disappointed in President Bush and scared of what the future holds. Elizabeth says, "I want the Iraq war to work, but I'm afraid it won't. The war on terrorism will go on and on and on." Kip puts the blame squarely on President Bush, ranking him right up there with Hitler as a villain of historic proportions. Still, she says she supports the American troops, and she does not favor an immediate military withdrawal from Iraq. Only Will and Nadine, the two youngest people in the group, were opposed to the war from the beginning. They've seen little to change their minds since then.

In the coming chapters we'll look in more detail at each of these people's dreams. Using the same basic approach we've just used with Dan and Sophia, we'll explore the connections between their dream contents and their waking-life beliefs regarding other "hot-button" political issues. Many additional layers of meaning could be explored, of course, and nothing I'm saying should be taken as ruling out other possible interpretations. Every dream has multiple dimensions of significance; there is never a single correct interpretation. I invite readers to visit my Web site and explore the dreams for themselves. Several of the focus group members agreed to allow their journals to be posted online for study and comment, and you may discover themes in their dreams that I've overlooked in this book. If so, I look forward to hearing about it.

3

Religion, Spirituality, and Faith

To understand the psychological roots of American politics we
need to look beyond issues of war and terrorism. People's feelings about the war are part of a larger tapestry of beliefs that
includes their views on morality, good and evil, faith, and God—
religious beliefs, in other words, which for many people represent their core life convictions. In this chapter we'll explore the
dreams of conservatives and liberals as a way of illuminating the
connections between their political and religious principles. Each
of the dream journal keepers described their religious beliefs and
feelings to me in considerable detail, and I sifted through their
dreams for images and themes relating to their spiritual sentiments.
What emerges in the patterns of their dreams is striking testimony
to the continuing power of religion in American politics, not just
at the level of campaign rhetoric or election slogans but in people's
actual experiences of personal faith and ultimate meaning.

Religious Liberty

America is, and has always been, a passionately religious nation.
Many of the earliest Europeans who journeyed across the At-

lantic to the New World were driven by a desire to worship God as they chose, without any external interference or coercion. For them, the American Dream meant a chance to purify and intensify their religious devotion beyond what was possible in their countries of origin. In the scattered colonies they and other European immigrants built along the eastern seaboard in the seventeenth and eighteenth centuries, they experimented with different forms of governance aimed at defending religious liberty. When they joined together to form a single nation, they placed their affirmation of this principle in a uniquely central location —the first sentence of the First Amendment to the Constitution: "Congress shall make no law respecting an establishment of religion, or prohibiting the free exercise thereof." Within that wide, constitutionally protected space, Americans have followed their religious callings in an astonishing variety of different directions. They've become swept up in fervent revivals and "great awakenings," embraced a seemingly endless series of new prophets, preachers, and visionaries, and spread their worship practices and ritual celebrations to every corner of the national map.

For the most part, all this religious activity has occurred within a Christian context. The people in those original colonies were almost entirely Christians, and every one of the writers of the Constitution was at least nominally a Christian. In the earliest days of the nation, the term *religious freedom* effectively meant the freedom to adopt some version of Christian faith. That's no longer the case, as the United States is now home to growing populations of Muslims, Buddhists, Hindus, Jews, and members of many other non-Christian religions. Nevertheless, the character of the nation has remained primarily Christian. In America today, 85 percent of the people follows some version of the Christian faith. More than half the population considers religion to be "very important" in their lives. Eighty-one percent of Americans believe in heaven, 69 percent believe in hell.[1] Fully 95 percent of

Americans believe in the existence of God or a higher power; only 5 percent believe in nothing beyond the physical world.[2]

The Religion Gap

Any doubt about religion's importance in American politics should have ended with the 2000 and 2004 presidential elections. The results of those contests revealed a sizable "religion gap" between the Republican and Democratic parties.[3] People who said they regularly attended church voted 60 percent for George W. Bush and only 40 percent for Al Gore. Among those who attend church more than weekly, the 2004 electoral split was 65 percent for Bush, 35 percent for Kerry. Bush did significantly better with voters concerned about "moral values" than did Kerry, and white evangelical Protestants (more than a quarter of all Americans) overwhelmingly favored Bush and the Republican Party. Over the past several election cycles a strong polarization has developed among America's religious communities—each political party now has its own "religious base." White evangelicals, conservative Christians, and Mormons are extremely reliable Republican voters, while black Protestants, nonwhite Catholics (e.g., Latinos), Jews, and the religiously unaffiliated vote in large majorities for the Democrats. In 2000 and 2004 the religious swing voters were white Protestants from mainline denominations (Presbyterians, Methodists, Episcopalians, etc.) and white Catholics. A big reason Bush won both elections is because he persuaded those voters that the Republicans were more attuned to their religious ideals and moral concerns than were the Democrats.

Since then the Democrats have labored mightily to prove to religious Americans that they, too, are a party of faith. The 2006 congressional elections showed some success in that effort, improving the Democrats' showing among people who attend church once a week or more, with greater support across nearly all Christian groups. Less widely reported but also notable, the

Democrats made large gains in the 2006 elections among voters who attend church less than weekly, and also among those who are not affiliated with any religious group.[4] The increasingly close connection between the Republican Party and conservative Christianity seems to have prompted a backlash in which growing numbers of mildly religious and nonreligious Americans are gravitating toward the Democrats. To the extent that more and more Americans are describing themselves as "spiritual but not religious," this could become a surprising factor in the 2008 elections. The "religion gap" may still favor the Republicans, but a "*non*religion" gap seems to be opening to the advantage of the Democrats.

All of this evidence suggests that the political psychologies of conservatives and liberals are thoroughly intertwined with their personal attitudes toward religion. Whatever people do or do not believe about religion has a direct bearing on their political views.

Religious and Spiritual Dimensions of Dreaming

Of all the subtopics covered in the book, this one is supported by the most substantial body of dream research material. Psychologists, historians, anthropologists, and theologians have been studying the religious and spiritual dimensions of dreaming for many decades.[5] While numerous questions remain to be answered, a few important facts about dreams and religion have been firmly established, and we can use two in particular as guides in this chapter.

First, dreaming is as close as anything could be to a universal feature of religion. From the ancient teachings of India, China, Egypt, and Greece to the indigenous traditions of Africa, Oceania, and the Americas, from the shamanistic practices of Neolithic cave dwellers to the global religions of Christianity, Islam, and Buddhism, dreams have consistently played a variety of important roles (e.g., revealing prophetic wisdom, healing illness and suffering, inspiring creative new forms of worship, communicating with ancestors). Not every person experiences dreams with explicit references to religion, but traditions all over the world have looked to dreams as authentic portals into the realm of whatever the given culture considers sacred or divine. The implication for our project is that anything we discover about the spiritually meaningful dreams of the focus group members should be considered in light of the religious dreaming tendencies of humankind—each individual is expressing in her or his own way a dream potential that's latent in the psyches of all people. Putting the same point slightly differently, it shouldn't be considered odd, superstitious, or unscientific to examine the religious aspects of dreaming. On the contrary, studying those religious aspects is the most reasonable and historically grounded way of exploring the full impact of dreams on people's lives.

The second fact to keep in mind is that the continuity principle I described in chapter 1 extends to religious beliefs, practices, and experiences. Whatever is most religiously important to a person in waking life is very likely to be reflected in his or her dreams. For most people the frequency of explicitly religious dreams tends to be low, but those few dreams can provide surprisingly accurate portrayals of the individual's feelings and concerns about religion in waking life. A couple years ago, as part of a class I was teaching on the psychology of dreaming, I asked a group of students to analyze blindly (i.e., without any extra personal information) a series of dreams recorded by a young woman who donated the series to a dream research Web site and who agreed to respond to questions about her dreams. By doing nothing more than reading and word searching the dream series, the students were able to make specific predictions about her religious upbringing and current beliefs—namely, that she was not raised in a religious family and now considers herself a spiritual person who feels a positive connection with God. When we asked the young woman to describe her past and present views about religion, she confirmed the students' predictions about her lack of a church background and her strong but still rather form-less spiritual yearnings. This neatly demonstrates the value of dream analysis as a tool in the study of personal religious beliefs. I want to emphasize that the students did not need any Freudian or Jungian concepts to make their predictions; all they did was read the dreams and identify basic patterns in the appearance of various elements. This means that as long as we stay close to clearly identifiable patterns of dream content, we can be reason-ably confident in making inferences about the psychological roots of people's religious and spiritual lives.

Conservative Visions

Let's go back to the dreams of Dan and Sophia and see what we learn by studying the frequency patterns in light of their religious beliefs. In Dan's case, we find an immediate *dis*continuity—his dreams include no explicit mention of religion, yet he was raised as a Catholic and went to church regularly through his teenage years. There are two possible explanations for this. One, the total number of dreams in Dan's series (thirty-one) may be too small for the frequency patterns that would signal his Catholic upbringing to emerge. Two, the lack of religious content in his dreams may in fact be consistent with a lack of strong religious feelings in his current waking life. The first explanation is certainly plausible, and I would predict that if we gathered more dreams from Dan, and dreams from less battle-stressed times of his life, we'd be likely to find some references to his early Catholicism. But the second explanation makes most sense in light of Dan's own re-sponses to questions about religion. He does not consider himself an especially religious person at this point in his life. He's not highly emotional or talkative about his beliefs, he rarely attends worship services (other than funerals), and he's never had what he considers a religious experience. It's fair to say that religion is not a major preoccupation in Dan's waking life, and his dreams appear to be accurate reflections of that.

But Dan says he remains a Catholic in outlook, particularly in regards to the church's moral teachings on marriage, abortion, and contraception. These teachings form the bedrock of conservative Christianity in present-day America, and it's worth noting the obvious fact that they all relate to the theme of defending the traditional family. As we saw in the previous chapter, Dan's dreams often revolved around that "family-in-danger" theme. A concern about family safety represents a strong motivational factor in Dan's life that shapes both his political and religious perspectives. The most enduring part of his Catholic upbringing has been its ideal of a faithful, prosperous nuclear family, and his support of President Bush and the Republicans goes beyond the war to his agreement with their strong stands on "family values" (not surprisingly, Dan felt a hearty dislike for Bill Clinton).

For the most part, Dan's dreams mirror those basic beliefs and play them out in mundane, realistic, this-worldly settings. He's a no-nonsense guy in the waking world, and he's a no-nonsense guy in his dreams, too. Indeed, his dream series is so devoid of bizarreness, emotion, and general dreaming chaos that it's tempting to view him as a dull or uncreative person. That would be unfair, though. Dan (and probably many other conservatives) expresses his creativity in ways that are true and specific to his personal ideals. Here's where a single dream can tell us something important. On the third night of the journaling process Dan recorded two dreams (the only other time he recorded two dreams in a single night was the night of the "War" dreams, discussed in the previous chapter). The first of these dreams involves a lengthy and frustrating scene at his unit's command center, where he struggles to do his work while other soldiers are behav-

ing in confused and unprofessional ways. That's followed by this
dream:

> I'm walking by some big military tents at night. I look in-
> side of one and there's a woman. She has an electrical wire
> or cord in her hands—one cord with two wires sticking
> out, their bare ends exposed. I stopped because the ends of
> the wires were glowing and she was looking at the glow
> of this tiny light, right next to her eyes, like she was trans-
> fixed or mesmerized by it, bringing it closer and closer. I
> stopped, thinking, "What the heck?" I was going to walk
> up and ask "What are you doing?" but the dream ended. I
> felt puzzled, but no fear. It was a strange sight.

Of all the dreams in Dan's series, this is the only one with any
qualities that might be termed "mystical." Visions of beautiful,
alluring brilliance have been reported in cultures all over the
world, and most religious traditions have recognized light as a
symbol of divine energy. The fact that it's a woman holding the
light suggests a connection to his wife, Sophia, whose interest
in feminine spirituality we'll discuss in a moment. The electrical
cord comes from Dan's military base; but inside the tent it's *her*
world, *her* reality, an eerie realm he doesn't quite understand
("What the heck?") but feels drawn to explore.

It could be just a coincidence, but this dream of a little spark
of light appearing inside an enclosed feminine space occurred
about a month after Sophia conceived their second child, and the
day before they learned the results of her pregnancy test. In
the comparative study of religions we would call this a "conception dream," a dream heralding the birth of a child, something
that's found in many cultural traditions around the world.[6] Such
dreams are especially common among women but are also reported by men. If a politically and religiously conservative soldier

like Dan were ever going to experience something as spiritually extraordinary as a precognitive dream, it makes sense that it would focus on conception and new life, revealing a true vision of the creative brilliance of his about-to-expand family.

The Goddess

Turning to Sophia, we discover right away that she breaks the stereotype of political conservatives being conservative in their religious beliefs, too. That's true with Dan, but not for Sophia. By any measure, she's remarkably liberal in her religious perspective. She was raised Catholic but doesn't attend worship services any longer, and she openly admits that she's doubting her past beliefs. She does her best to avoid confrontations with the "Saturday door-knocker" Christians from their army base community who sweep through the neighborhood each weekend aggressively proselytizing on behalf of their churches. When they arrive at your door, Sophia says, "You have to be prepared to defend yourself, or lie." Although her support for President Bush marks her as conservative, she is nothing less than a flaming liberal in the realm of religion. Her strongest religious feelings derive from two decidedly non-Christian sources: her belief in ancient goddesses and figures of divine femininity, and her feelings of kinship with Native American spirituality. She knows she has to be very careful about revealing her true beliefs, lest she become known in town as a heretic who needs more vigorous attention from the door-knockers. Dreams have long played an integral role in her spiritual life ("I always had very vivid dreams as a child"), and her answer to the "most memorable dream" question is a good example of how dreams can sometimes become a medium of religious transformation, almost like a personal ritual of initiation. This dream occurred a couple of years earlier, during what Sophia described as "the hardest time of my life." Her first child was a year old, Dan was deployed overseas, and her very conservative Catholic family had been pressuring her to give up her unorthodox ways and return to the church. A few nights after a particularly upsetting phone conversation with her sister, she dreamed this:

> I am watching the sky with another woman (a mother of a friend of mine); we are in a forest clearing. I see a huge black hawk flying toward us. She has one white feather attached to her right wing. The feather has two red stripes with a turquoise stripe between. Her wingspan could reach eight to ten feet easily, as a huge vulture. Upon touching the ground her wings expand and stretch behind her. She suddenly, divinely shape-shifts into a tall beautiful woman. The shape-shift was nothing short of divine, no words to describe. It was Godlike. She stood before me in a long, white, tight-fitted dress, strapless and muslinlike. Her hair is black, pulled tight to her head. She says to me, "I am Yaqeen, I am Yaqeen." She wills me to repeat, which I do.

Sophia spent several years of her childhood living in a remote desert region of Arizona, and she says "my Catholic upbringing in this small Mexican/Apache town was full of mysticism... angel appearances and so forth." This dream could certainly qualify as an angelic visitation, though there's nothing particularly Christian about it. It's much closer to the kinds of dreams Native American cultures seek when they perform vision quest rituals. Such dreams are desired because they can bring the individual into relation with a powerful spirit being who will become that person's lifelong guide and companion. Sophia feels just that way about the goddess figure, who represents for her the profoundly mysterious power of women in the world, and whose presence in her personal life has been a constant source of reassurance.

Yaqeen is an Arabic word for "certainty" or "truth." Sophia had studied some Arabic in hope of better understanding what her husband was experiencing in Iraq, but she doesn't recall ever consciously learning that particular word. She said when she looked it up after waking, the word made perfect sense to her as an emblem of her determination to remain true to her own core spiritual beliefs. The dream's imagery unleashed a flood of associations to mythic birds—the Crow and Hawk spirits of Native American lore, and Ma'at, the ancient Egyptian goddess with vulture wings who weighs the hearts of the dead to judge their souls' worthiness to enter the afterlife. Rather than bowing to the external pressures of religious conformity, Sophia chose to believe in her dream's inner revelation of truth and spiritual transformation.

Once we understand these qualities of her most memorable dream and their relations to her spiritual life, we gain a much sharper insight into the particular nature of Sophia's politically conservative views. When asked what she didn't like about Bill Clinton, she pointed specifically to his disrespect for women. When asked what she did like about George W. Bush, she mentioned his efforts in "bringing women leaders to the forefront" of his administration, particularly Condoleezza Rice. For Sophia it's a conservative virtue to affirm and respect the power of women, including but not restricted to the power of bearing children. From her perspective the Democrats don't care enough about the degradation of women in society, while the Republicans show greater concern for women's dignity and honor. A politician wanting to get Dan's vote would make a straightforward appeal to family values and military security. A politician wanting to win over Sophia would do best by going beyond family values to emphasize women's leadership and the importance of feminine energy. If a conservative politician ever spoke up on behalf of environmental stewardship and Native American rights,

Sophia would probably do cartwheels on her way to signing up as a campaign volunteer.

Let's turn now to her dream series. Sophia kept the journal for a little more than a year and, as we've noted, recorded a total of 276 dreams. Taking into account the fact that she made very few journal entries in November and December, the weeks immediately before and after the birth of her baby, her overall recall rate for the year was very close to one dream per night. That's on the high end of the recall spectrum, underscoring her claim that she's been a frequent and vivid dreamer since childhood. The fact that her reports are much longer than Dan's raises a methodological question: how much of a dream report's word length is a function of the individual's descriptive style? Researchers debate this, but I believe in Sophia's case it's not just a matter of her being excessively detailed or verbose—there's a lot going on in her dreams, and numerous words are required to describe it all. Well over half her dreams include some kind of bizarre, unrealistic, counterfactual occurrence, a further indication of her highly active dreaming imagination.

Family members appeared in nearly half of her dreams, a much higher percentage than is found in most people's dreams but entirely consistent with her personal circumstances and current waking-life concerns. Animals were present in 19 percent of her dreams, again much higher than average. Some studies have suggested that pregnant women dream more frequently of animals (perhaps as metaphorical expressions for the growing life within them).[7] With Sophia, that aspect of dream animals seems to combine with her sense of divine feminine energies as moving fluidly between animal and human forms.

Intriguingly, Sophia's dream series lacks several elements often considered the hallmarks of "big" or "extraordinary" dreaming. During the journal-keeping year Sophia reported no flying dreams, no dreams of lucidity or being able to control things, and only a couple of character metamorphoses. Apparently, those aren't directions in which her dreaming capacities have developed. Instead, her dreams tend to thrust her in strange and confusing situations in which she struggles to understand what's happening and how to accomplish her goals. Although she's never lucid per se, Sophia's mental abilities are highly activated in her dreams as she reflects on her predicaments, thinks about different possibilities, analyzes other people's behavior, and makes plans for future actions. This seems to me the main reason she doesn't suffer nightmares or negative emotions more often in her dreams, which frequently open with nightmarelike scenarios (e.g., being lost, confronting strange animals, coming into contact with threatening people). Sophia has a remarkable ability to manage problems and overcome difficulties in her dreams, and in this she and Dan are surprisingly alike. Qualities of self-possession, focus, and "coolness under fire" pervade each of their dream series. These are attributes both of them embody in their waking lives, and it's something they look for in their political leaders, too.

Liberal Christianity

It's time to expand the conversation beyond Sophia and Dan to include those focus group members of a more liberal persuasion. A majority of Christians may be conservative Republicans, but many other Christians are liberal Democrats, and their voices should be included in any worthwhile analysis of what it means to be liberal in contemporary America. Elizabeth is a great example of a faithful, churchgoing Christian who favors the Democrats. She was raised in rural Kentucky by conservative parents who were active members of the local Independent Christian Church. They divorced in the early 1960s when Elizabeth was a young teenager. The combination of her fractured family situation and the cultural changes of the sixties pushed her thinking far beyond the traditional beliefs of her childhood. The civil rights movement made a big impact on her as she became aware of the injustice of racism in her own community. Looking back at her life from the vantage of fifty-eight years, Elizabeth feels her view of the world has changed and broadened dramatically from what she was taught as a child. Like Sophia, she knows her beliefs represent an unwelcome minority in a predominantly conservative, "Bible-thumping" town, but she seems to feel energized by the conflict. Elizabeth belongs to a Disciples of Christ church in which she's been a leading member for many years (holding positions as church elder, financial committee member, and Sunday school teacher). What motivates her passionate commitment to the church is its open and inclusive message: "We welcome all." Elizabeth is still a Christian, but now she's become a *liberal* Christian who actively seeks opportunities to promote openness, tolerance, and inclusion.

The importance of religion in her life became evident in the first few entries of her dream journal. Three nights before Easter, when she was preparing for her various roles in the weekend's worship services, Elizabeth had this dream:

> Felt like I dreamed the same continuing dream all night. I was staying with friends and realized when I woke up that I had only sixty minutes to be dressed and at church to serve at the communion table for Easter services. I didn't have my clothes or makeup with me and couldn't get home to get them. I left my friends' house. My plan was to take a shower, wash my hair, and wear a liturgist robe. We had trouble (road problems, traffic, cars stopping) getting there. Finally we got there, with only fifteen minutes to spare. From that point on everything was mixed up—I couldn't find a shower, couldn't find anyone to help or a phone to call my husband so he could serve for me. Every-

where I went people couldn't give me the time even after looking at their watches. Somehow I ended up inside a different church, got lost, couldn't get out.

I suspect most readers have experienced similar nightmares of endless misfortune and frustrating difficulties. Such dreams usually express anxieties related to an important situation in waking life, and in Elizabeth's case she was in fact quite concerned about how well she would perform at the Easter service. She still hadn't decided what to wear, nor did she have all the details yet about what she was expected to do. Her dream can be seen as a mild version of a threat simulation nightmare, insofar as it catalogs in painful detail all the things that could wrong when the big celebration actually occurs. Easter is the holiest day of the Christian faith, and Elizabeth's desire to play her part well in the ritual drama was reflected in an emotionally negative but vividly memorable and attention-grabbing nightmare.

Over the course of the journaling year Elizabeth's sleep tended to be short (six to seven hours a night) and fairly good (aided by sleep medications), but bouts of extremely poor and disrupted sleeping plagued her every couple weeks. Her dream recall average was about one dream every two nights, with one nightmare every week or so. Her dream reports were usually quite lengthy, at least a hundred words and often three hundred or more, and about half of them included some kind of bizarrely unrealistic event. She experienced several visitation dreams from her deceased father, and for a woman nearing sixty years of age she had a remarkable number of sexual dreams, including those of a culturally and religiously taboo nature:

The girl suggested that perhaps I'd like to meet her in her bedroom after my shower. I got her message and told her that I had never done that. She said perhaps I would like to try. I told her yes.

79

In waking life Elizabeth is heterosexual, but the openness she feels in this dream to the possibility of a homosexual experience is consistent with her personal religious ideals. She's especially proud of her church's outreach efforts to the local gay and lesbian community, a policy that's deliberately aimed at countering the antigay rhetoric of the fundamentalist majority where she lives.

Knowing this about her dreams helps explain why Elizabeth is justified in considering herself "very liberal" in political terms. When she first told me this I was skeptical—I live next door to the People's Republic of Berkeley, I *know* what very liberal people look like, and Elizabeth (who voted for Bush in 2004 and opposes limitations on gun owner rights) didn't fit the profile. But looking at her dreams and their relation to her religious life, it becomes clear that what makes Elizabeth a genuine liberal is her profound belief in the virtue of equality and her personal experience of growing beyond the racial and sexual prejudices of her community. A powerful theme in her waking *and* dreaming life has been learning to expand her understanding of people who appear different. Compared to most residents in her area, Elizabeth is very liberal indeed.

I asked Elizabeth what she thought of America's current political situation, and she sighed and paused for several moments. "I'm so confused about where our country is, and where it's going," she finally said. She went on to describe several local political scandals that she felt reflected a deeper corruption found at all levels of government. Even politicians she has voted for have utterly failed (she now puts President Bush in that category), and she perceives a severe lack of leadership in the country. "I'm proud to be an American," she declared, "but come on, guys, let's wake up and deal with the real problems we're facing." What would she do to make things better? "Give everyone a 'Get it together, folks' pill. Start with the politicians and religious leaders and work your way down through state/local governments, schools, places of work, homes. Perhaps what America needs now is a strong dose of the Golden Rule."

So here's a Christian whose egalitarian religious ideals prompt her to favor mostly liberal, mostly Democratic political positions. She's not a yellow dog Democrat, not an absolutely reliable part of the base—"I'll go Republican if I like who's running better" —but she's strongly attracted to politicians who articulate the ideals of openness and tolerance that are so personally important to her. "I think a lot of Lincoln," she told me, "He was ahead of his time on many issues related to fairness and equality. He stuck his neck out to do the right thing." As far as Elizabeth can see, there are no leaders today with such powers of visionary courage. But she's still hoping to find one.

One Nation under God

It's no surprise that Paul's dreams frequently refer to religion. As a former Catholic priest, he spent the first forty-nine years of his life completely celibate and devoted to the church in body, mind, and soul. The influence of his career in the clergy contin- ues to reverberate in his dreams, even though he long ago made his peace with the decision to leave the priesthood. Here's what he reported in reply to my question about his most recent dream:

> I was in an unfamiliar chapel and I felt alone. I was saying Mass. I was wearing old clothes (like jeans, a T-shirt, etc.). It got to the point of the offertory and I became conscious that people were there with me and most of them were priests (unfamiliar to me). I began feeling guilty that I wasn't in vestments, so I stopped Mass and went to dress. I continued Mass.

Paul no longer wears the priestly robes in waking life, yet he says he remains a faithful Catholic. His primary spiritual struggle, as represented in this dream, revolves around staying true to his own relationship with God while finding some way to respect the traditions of the Catholic faith. Paul received many expressions of displeasure and disapproval from his colleagues when he gave up his vows to marry a nun and start a family, and as a result he was forced to create his own spiritual path in the latter half of his life. The difficulty of this task appears in nightmarish form in what Paul says was the most memorable dream of his life, a short but vivid recurrent dream that started when he left the priesthood:

> I am in a corridor of some sort and am not able to get out of it. I keep looking for ways out.

The frequency of the dream has tapered off in recent years (it did not appear in his journal), but Paul says that for ten years following his departure from the church he experienced this same disturbing nightmare at least two or three times a month. In the dreams he recorded in the journal (136 total over the course of twelve months), some reference to religion appears in a fifth of them, consistent with his past experiences and present concerns. However, Paul reported very few dreams that could be considered genuine nightmares. Only a handful of his dreams included strong emotions of fear, helplessness, or vulnerability. This apparently represents a significant change in Paul's dream life, indicating that he has indeed come to terms with his religious past —he's finally found his way out of the nightmare corridor, and he now feels more confident about God's presence in his life and the world.

Other than an unusually high percentage of references to religion, Paul's sleep and dream patterns are most remarkable for their steadiness and simplicity. Only four nights during the whole year did he report anything less than a good night's sleep. His reports were consistently brief, mostly in the 50- to 100-word range, with just four dreams in the series requiring more than 150 words to describe. His journal entries included relatively few emotions or feelings, no flying dreams, one brief lucid dream, and only a few other dreams with magical events or good fortunes. More than two-thirds of Paul's dreams were mundane, portraying realistic settings and familiar interactions. Of the bizarre dreams he did report, they usually involved strange shifts in his age (e.g., being a child or a young man) or occupation (e.g., working as a football coach or a truck driver). For the most part Paul's dreams revolved around the familiar themes of religion, teaching (he worked for ten years as a school administrator after leaving the priesthood), and his family (he enjoys close relationships with his ex-wife and his four children). His behavior and thought processes in his dreams were usually competent and controlled, and he experienced little of the fantastic, monstrous, or uncanny that haunts the sleep of so many other people.

In all these ways, Paul fits the profile of the "conservative dreamer" as discussed in chapter 1. He sleeps soundly and consistently, and his dreams tend to be less varied and more mundane. This finding is consistent with the waking-world fact that Paul's political views have been moving in a conservative direction as well. He says, "I've been through all the liberal concepts, and I'm sick of them." Although a lifelong Democrat, Paul's strong beliefs about "life issues" (i.e., opposing abortion), his support for the Iraq war, and his disgust with lying politicians (e.g., Bill Clinton) have pushed him more and more into the conservative Republican camp. A "compulsive watcher of Fox news," Paul believes the country would benefit from greater cooperation between the government and religious groups. He thinks the separation of church and state has been taken to an unhealthy extreme: "We all believe in the same God. Why can't we find unity?" If politicians could just stop arguing and talk to each other like humans, he feels, they would find their shared religious ideals are much more important than their partisan differences. One of the dreams Paul reported during the year of journaling illustrated in very literal terms his faith in the ultimate goal of national unity:

> I am participating in a huge political rally. What is different about this rally is that it is made up of both Democrats and Republicans, and this is what is most unusual: everyone is getting along and agreeing with each other.

Talk about a bizarre dream! Humans may develop the magical power to fly before such a happy political communion will ever come to pass. And yet the hope Paul expresses in this dream is real and important, not only for him but for the nation—without more people committing to national values that transcend party politics, America's future prospects are bleak. Although Paul has become quite liberal and unorthodox in his spiritual beliefs ("ordinary people are so prayerful... There are mystics all around us"), his political perspective today is strongly conservative in calling for a new American unity grounded in religion, in people's shared faith in a single, all-powerful and all-loving God. President Bush and the Republican Party appeal to Paul for exactly this reason, and his alienation from the Democrats is due in large part to their secularist policies. Still, as the 2008 elections approach, Paul's desire is for a presidential candidate from either party who will talk openly and honestly with Americans about the common religious faith that binds them into one great nation.

Atheism

Defined in this way, Paul's vision of unity does not include the small group of Americans who reject the tenets of all religious traditions. Atheists constitute about 5 percent of the population, and their presence in the national community raises tough questions. Are people in this country free *not* to worship God? Can a nation founded by Christians accept as true members those people who have no religious faith whatsoever? How far is the state required to go in accommodating atheists and their convictions —must all religious references be banished from official business and public celebrations? For the most part atheists are tolerated in contemporary America, though their legal efforts to remove the phrases "In God We Trust" from U.S. currency and "under God" from the Pledge of Allegiance have earned them the scorn of talk radio conservatives. In a recent poll on the religious characteristics American voters could accept in a president, being an atheist was at the very bottom of the list—people say they would be more likely to vote for a Jew, a Mormon, or even a Muslim before they'd vote for an atheist.[8]

The group of dream journal keepers included two people, Will and Kip, who separated themselves from all forms of religion, though Kip's views could be considered spiritual in reference to belief in some kind of higher power or intelligence. We'll consider her story in more detail in the next chapter. Will seems to be more classically atheist in finding no use for any religious or spiritual precepts. He was raised Catholic, but as he grew up and began thinking for himself he found the teachings of Christianity falling woefully short in comparison to the objective findings of science. Possessed of a brilliant mind with skills in math, physics, philosophy, and literature (no one else in the focus group reported dreams involving Dostoyevsky, Oscar Wilde, quantum physics, or number theory), Will considers religion an unnecessary emotional crutch. He understands why, for example, his mother finds comfort and solace in her Catholic faith, and he's happy for her, but he personally puts his trust in science to teach the truth about life's realities. What most struck me when talking with

Will about his atheism was its *non*rebellious nature. Far from a bomb-throwing anarchist, Will is a gentle young man who is devoted to his family and who took it upon himself a couple years ago to be the primary caregiver for his ailing grandmother during the final two weeks of her life. His atheism isn't about attacking or refuting the religious beliefs of his family. Will feels he's simply outgrown them.

It's hard to evaluate Will's dreams with the methods I've been using so far. Will has suffered a few episodes in his life of severe mental distress requiring professional care, and his dreams clearly reflect an unusually turbulent and hyperactive imagination. Out of concern for his privacy I did not ask Will for more information about his experiences with psychotherapy, and thus I don't know how much of his dreaming is attributable to those factors.

The earliest dream Will can remember came when he was around four years old, and its water theme has been a prominent feature throughout his dreaming life:

> I'm at the aquarium, and my dad is towering over me. Some other kids from preschool are there. Dad picks me up and puts me on his shoulders. I look into the tank of lionfish. Then I look at the dolphin tank. I see "Buster" the dolphin. I realize in the dream that the air is like water. I feel a weightlessness. I go around swimming up the stairwell and hovering there. I awaken with a very enchanted feeling.

In the first interview Will gave for this project, he was asked to describe his most recent dream, and this is what he reported:

> This is a recurring dream: I am at the beach where my family and I vacation every summer in real life. I am walking down wooden steps from the cottage. The sand is very

fine beneath me. I walk into the water. The water is wavy because it's a blustery kind of day in the summer. The air currents are filling my ear. I feel the spray from the water hitting the breakers near my ankles. I look back and it appears I'm a mile from the cabin but I feel as if I've only walked thirty yards or so. I hit a sandbar and all of a sudden, the sea calms. At that moment, one unitary cell catches me. I am riding this wave as it increases. I feel like I'm a thousand feet over the cabin now. I can feel everything from the wind at my face to the water beneath me. Nothing on the ground is being destroyed, even though the water is traveling over the top of it.

Will said these recurrent dreams verged on being nightmares because they were so vivid, perplexing, and repetitive. As first mentioned in chapter 2, such experiences can be called "titanic dreams" because of the way they evoke an intense feeling of interaction with the elemental powers and primal forces of nature. By my count, Will had twenty titanic dreams out of the total of ninety-six he recorded during his year of journal keeping, a far higher proportion than I found in any of the other nine participants. Along with massive waves and vast expanses of water, he dreamed of traveling through space, merging with light, dissolving into particles, and slowing down the passage of time —continuous, in a way, with his waking-life fascination with physics, but extremely discontinuous with the ordinary boundaries of human perception and experience.

Will's sleeping patterns tended to be erratic and troubled, with multiple nights of five or fewer hours of sleep. More than half the time he said his sleep quality was only fair or poor. His dream recall frequency (about two a week) was moderate compared to others in the group, and his reports were not especially long (two-thirds were 125 words or fewer). But by almost any measure Will's dreams were extremely bizarre, with a multitude of fantastic settings, magical events, and transcendental insights. In dreaming his mind seemed to reach out for larger realities than could be encompassed in his quotidian waking life—a boundary-crossing impulse that often led to terrifying nightmares of being stranded and alone. But along with the frightening dreams came fantastic visions that might, in a different context, be considered mystical experiences, such as these two:

I am a tiny droplet of water. First I'm brushed along the currents of Lake Superior. I can see tall cliffs, I feel the cold, deep dark oligotrophic [adverse to life] cold. In Michigan I pass the dunes, and am sucked into space by a large wave. The wave begins similar to my recurring dream, but in this one I'm a droplet, and I'm being shot into space, through the troposphere, the stratosphere, the ionosphere, feeling the cold, the heat, and then the cold. I see a Whiting Event [a comic book reference] over Lake Michigan. I feel a sense of isolation—a drop from the sea traveling away from earth into space. I can barely make out our sun, then I evaporate, as I am thrown into a big star like Antares. I feel dissociated, my consciousness at different points in time and space. Then I wake.

I'm on a lawn chair at my grandma's house. She and I are drinking milkshakes while watching a sunset. She's reading me one of her poems, "Little Miss Nobody." As she reads, I shift time and space to the church where I'm eulogizing her. I can see the faces of my extended family. I hear Grandma reading again and look over at her chair, but she's not there. I'm crying. The sun burns out over the gorge. I wake up.

People who are political conservatives may have dreams like these, but according to my research, people who are politically liberal tend to have more of them. The reason may be that people who frequently experience amazing dream visions and terrifying nightmares are primed to value the creativity of the human mind and to be sensitive to any efforts to constrain its powers. Will is a liberal Democrat who strongly disapproves of President Bush. He has been opposed to the Iraq war from the start, and he wants much more governmental support for public education. His strongest political feelings right now are disappointment and anger at the Republican Party for rejecting the life-saving benefits of science (e.g., stem cell research) and for demonizing gays and lesbians. As far as he's concerned, the whole political system needs an overhaul, with "more visionaries in office" who will institute "policies for *all* people, not just the powerful few." Will's atheism, his intense dreaming, and his political views are all psychologically connected—they're grounded in his personal experiences of the mind's tremendous powers of insight and understanding. He's frustrated by his own inability to focus his mental energies, and he's aware of being an unusual person well outside the mainstream of his community. Nevertheless, his highest ideal both personally and politically is freedom of thought, and in that regard he's as authentically American as anyone else. Will favors the Democrats because they express greater respect for individual differences, more trust in the objective findings of scientific research, and more concern for fully funded, high-quality schools where people can learn to reason and think for themselves. He'll probably remain a loyal Democrat as long as the party continues to uphold these values and doesn't go too far in accommodating the moral concerns of conservative Christians.

Church versus Dreaming

The sleep and dreams frequency poll included a question about how often the respondents attend religious services. This is a typical survey question used to gauge the strength of people's religious commitments, and in this case it yielded results broadly consistent with other demographic studies. In all, 40 percent of the country attend worship services at least once a week, 26 percent at least a few times each year, and 31 percent rarely or never. I thought the most interesting contrast arose between the two extremes, those who go to a religious service more than once a week versus those who never attend.

Religious Attendance and Sleep Patterns

Sleep patterns		More than once a week (%)	Never (%)
Duration	Fewer than 6 hours a night	11	18
	6–8.9 hours a night	84	76
	More than 9 hours a night	2	6
Insomnia	Never	70	51
	1–2 nights a week	13	19
	3 or more nights a week	13	27

Religious Attendance and Dream Patterns

Dream type	More than once a week (%)	Never (%)
A person who's now dead appearing alive	29	41
Magically flying in the air	25	29
Being chased or attacked	33	45
Falling	40	44
Sexual experiences	34	50
Being in a situation exactly like your regular waking life	53	63
Being aware you're dreaming and able to control the dream	37	47

Most opinion polls in recent years have shown a correlation between the most intense religious worshippers and the most loyal supporters of President Bush, matched by an equally strong connection between nonreligious people and anti-Bush sentiment. My poll adds to that finding by showing that the differences we noted in chapter 1 between political conservatives and liberals also emerge when we compare the sleep and dream experiences of religious conservatives and liberals. Regular church attendees sleep longer and have fewer sleep troubles than those who never attend worship services. Nonreligious people report more of every type of dream, especially sexual dreams.

The implication is that being religious in America somehow has a dampening effect on dreaming (or at least on talking about dreams). The evidence at hand points to a psychologically conservative quality among the most active church members. This may be just what we'd expect based on our knowledge about the sleep and dream patterns of political conservatives. But it's contrary to the cross-cultural history of dreaming, in which religious traditions frequently encourage people to pay *more* attention to their dreams as valuable sources of inspiration and guidance. It would take us too far afield to delve into the various theological teachings in America's religious denominations, but I'll leave you with the suggestion that their collective impact on people's dreaming has moved in a constricting rather than expanding direction.[9] Simply put, American churches are not the friendliest places for dreaming. The biggest dreamers in the United States today tend to be those people least attached to a conventional religious group.

4

The Natural Environment

Over the past several decades, America's political sphere has developed an increasingly greenish hue. Issues of environmental protection are now a standard part of the national conversation about what our elected officials should or shouldn't do with the powers of the state. According to many polls, sizable majorities of the U.S. public say they want the government to act more vigorously to prevent global warming, clean up pollution, protect endangered animals, and develop new energy technologies.[1] A study in the fall of 2007 by Stanford University's Woods Institute for the Environment in collaboration with the Associated Press found that 84 percent of Americans want the president and Congress to do much more than they are currently doing to help the environment.[2] Many Republicans and almost all Democrats support greater collective effort to address the environmental problems that face us now and loom ahead in the future. Here, then, lies another area that's ripe for liberal-conservative integration. Across the ideological spectrum, Americans are deeply concerned about the well-being of the natural environment. They're looking for political leaders who will act intelligently, creatively, and decisively in reversing the environmental damage that's already been done and minimizing additional damage in the future.

Before delving into the sleep and dreaming dimensions of environmental awareness, let's pause to consider the historical fact that Americans did not begin with a caring, benevolent attitude toward nature. Far from it.

This Land Is Our Land

When Alexis de Tocqueville journeyed across the twenty-four states that comprised the American nation in 1831 he made several observations about the enthusiasm of its citizens for material gain and the accumulation of wealth. In his *Democracy in America* Tocqueville said many favorable things about the egalitarian ideals and self-directed spirit of American culture, but he admitted to finding the American people themselves rather dull and narrow-minded, with no interest in the beautiful glories of their natural surroundings:

> Europeans pay much attention to the wilds of America but Americans themselves scarcely ever think about them. The wonders of inanimate nature leave them cold and they may be said to ignore the marvelous forests around them until they fall to the axe. Another sight catches their gaze. The American people views its progress across these wilds, draining marshes, diverting rivers, peopling the open spaces, and taming nature. It is not just occasionally that this magnificent image of themselves captures the American imagination; it haunts every one of them in the slightest, as in the most important, of their actions, and ever floats before their minds.[3]

For the urbane Frenchman, America's wilderness offered a pleasurable opportunity for contemplative solitude, as far away from the densely populated cities of Europe as he could go. But he recognized that for Americans the natural environment held a very different meaning. To them it represented a source of raw material to be taken and used by anyone who wished to do so. At this formative stage in U.S. history, the consensus attitude toward nature focused almost entirely on control and domination. Animals, plants, minerals, lakes, rivers, forests—they were all considered freely available to those individuals who were intelligent and industrious enough to seize them and turn them into something humanly useful. As Tocqueville noted, the early Americans loved this "magnificent image" of themselves as the unfettered masters of nature, and it bound them together despite their many other political, religious, and social differences.[4]

This historical perspective helps explain the curious political question raised in chapter 1: why conservatives today are more likely than liberals to oppose efforts to care for the environment. This seems strange, given the great wilderness protection legacy of Republican president Theodore Roosevelt (1901–9) and the basic definition of conservatism as a political approach that tries to preserve traditional resources for future generations. The reason seems to be that conservatives want to conserve not nature, but people's freedom to own and control nature. They are primarily interested in protecting an earlier way of American life, when no one worried about the ecological consequences of their actions. Earlier Americans grew wealthy and prosperous by viewing the environment in this way, and present-day conservatives are understandably reluctant to give up a perspective that brings such personally enriching benefits.

For better or for worse, none of the ten journal keepers qualifies as that kind of conservative. All of them believe in the importance of laws and policies to protect against environmental damage that could end up resulting in severe harm to our country (not to mention the rest of the planet). They all recognize the complex interconnections between humans and the natural world, and they want politicians who will act more effectively to ensure the sustainable health of the environment. But as their dreams reveal, they approach environmental issues from very different psychological directions. In waking and in dreaming, there's more than one way to be an environmentalist.

Deep Ecology

We've already discussed a few examples of dreams that prominently feature aspects of nature. Will's visionary experience of being a water droplet (described in the previous chapter) involved an unusually intense immersion in a nonhuman aspect of the environment. Will said the dream reminded him of his childhood fascination with geography and astronomy, but that it also seemed to reveal something beyond his personal history: "I believe my being a water droplet was what the deep ecologist might call identifying with the greater whole: the idea that each of us is composed of matter that was once part of a lake, a star, everything."

It's hard not to see a direct connection between Will's perspective-stretching dream and his liberal political views about the environment. Many other liberals in contemporary America (particularly members of the Green Party) are also motivated by vivid feelings of empathy and kinship with the natural world. They may or may not be atheists like Will, but their spiritual beliefs often lead in decidedly non-Christian directions, very different from the orthodox religious practices of most people in the country (adding to the anxiety of conservatives, who accurately perceive a non-Christian belief system at work). This doesn't make Will or other greenish-liberals "un-American," however. Tocqueville may have said little about them, but early nineteenth-century New England transcendentalists like Ralph Waldo Emerson and Henry David Thoreau helped to develop an authentically American idea of nature as a portal into the divine, glorious in its transcendent power and freely available to all people. A strain of nature mysticism has run through our history ever since, with the writings of "deep ecologists" like John Muir, Aldo Leopold, and Annie Dillard expressing the views of a particular sort of American dreamer, one who values above all else the freedom of each and every human being, no matter how high or low in status, to enter into communion with the wilderness and wonder at its sacred vitality. Will's water droplet dream comes very close to the kind of experience Emerson recommended in his famed essay "On Nature": "Standing on the bare ground—my head bathed by the blithe air, and uplifted into infinite space—all mean egotism vanishes. I become a transparent eyeball; I am nothing; I see all; I am part or particle of God."[5] Whoever feels this way about nature is very likely to support political policies aimed at better care for the environment.

Does that mean greater ecological awareness automatically leads to a more liberal perspective? Not with Sophia, a political conservative who feels a strong bond with nature in both waking and dreaming life. In her "Yaqeen" dream she found herself receiving an important message from a hawk who magically transforms itself into a woman, an experience that intensified her already deep interest in Native American teachings about the sacred dimensions of the land and the majestic animals who share it with us. Sophia admitted that Yaqeen's message was theologically heretical—"basically she was telling me that my religion, within me, is ancient and goes farther back than Christianity." But what's most interesting in the present context is how Sophia's nature mysticism coexists with her conservative views on other political issues. This might be interpreted as one of the typical inconsistencies that arise when you ask people to explain their political beliefs. Yet for Sophia, a deep feeling of respect for nature reflects a truly conservative value, and she frankly questions why more Republicans don't appreciate the truth of that. She believes human life is most fulfilling when it's lived in harmony with, rather than in selfish opposition to, the natural world. The Native Americans knew this better than anyone, and Sophia regards their ideal as a genuinely conservative principle (that is, realistic and successfully tested by long experience) that can and should be applied in present-day America.

Animal Dreams

An easy way to evaluate the psychology of people's attitudes toward the environment is to study the presence and behavior of animals in their dreams. This approach has several advantages: (1) for many people, animals represent the most tangible form of nature they encounter in their waking lives; (2) animal characters are easy to count in dream reports, making for reliable findings of statistical frequency; and (3) many other studies (both quantitative and qualitative) have been done on animals in dreams, and the results open up interesting possibilities for comparative analysis.[6] Two of the journal keepers, Kip and Richard, had especially frequent contact with actual animals in their waking lives, and their dream series offer a window into the impact of the natural environment on their political views.

From one perspective, Kip is the embodiment of a classic American life. She's basically a cowboy, a westerner who spends her days working with horses on a ranch. Nothing better expresses the rugged individualism of American culture than the image of the cowboy riding on the open frontier. But from another perspective Kip is living far outside the mainstream of American morality, given her sexual orientation and family structure. Lesbian and gay rights are the subject of bitter disagreement in the contemporary United States, and Kip's sharply anti-Bush political views reflect her perception of the Republicans as unfairly biased against people like her—ordinary, hardworking people who love their children and simply want to be left alone.

We'll look at her work and family experiences in later chapters; for now, it's her dreams of animals and other natural phenomena that interest us. Her liberal ideals have deeper roots than just opposition to the war or anger at Republican homophobia. Recall her quip that she belongs to "the Church of the Living Hoof"— Kip's close physical work with horses provides her with a very tangible and grounded means of connecting with spiritual powers that fill her with a sense of deeper meaning and purpose. Horses, other animals, and forces of nature frequently appear in her dreams in ways that reveal higher truths (along with an endless stream of mundane frustrations). Close to half her dream reports include an animal character, an extremely high proportion compared to most people.[7] In many of Kip's animal dreams she's in the position of helping or caring for the creatures, which is also unusual in that most people's animal dreams tend to involve aggression and conflict. It's clear from her dreams that Kip spends much of her life in the company of animals, and her relations with them are mostly positive and respectful.

During the first month of keeping the dream journal, several storms dumped extraordinary amounts of rainfall on the area in northern California where Kip lives. Several of her dreams directly reflected these abnormal meteorological conditions:

> I remember dreaming about horses, fences, sitting in a corner of the fence and of course MUD—the bane of the winter of 2006.

For someone who trains horses, mud is more than an inconvenience; it's a serious health threat to the horses' feet. This waking-world concern had a clear impact on Kip's dreams, showing how sensitive dreaming can be to meaningful changes in the natural world.

Other than the high percentage of animal characters, Kip's dream patterns during the year of journal keeping were generally quite ordinary—she's more like Dan and Paul than Sophia and Will. Her sleep was good but on the short side, often seven or fewer hours a night. Most of her reports were in the range of seventy-five to one hundred words, and none of them was longer than three hundred words. Two-thirds of her dreams were mundane, portraying realistic situations from the ranch or her family. She reported no flying, no lucidity, and very few magical events. But her recall rate of five to six dreams per week was on the active end of the spectrum, and she experienced several truly bizarre dreams that involved a wide variety of fantastic changes to her perception of the world. Some of her most emotionally intense dreams involved animals, plants, and the personification of nature itself. For example, in a number of dreams Kip mourns for the death of her favorite horse, J, "a perfect and drop-dead gorgeous horse . . . He left a huge hole in my heart." She also had a distressing dream about the loss of a beloved cherry tree. When this particular tree, the best one on the ranch, unexpectedly died, Kip said she felt very sad and puzzled. A little while later she had this brief dream:

> I cut a bough off my cherry tree. Somehow it has men-
> strual blood on it. I put it in a vase.

The mourning for lost procreative power certainly resonates with Kip's personal experience as a post-child-bearing woman. But a level of individual meaning is not inconsistent with her feelings about the tree itself—in other words, the dream is not just about Kip's inner subjective world but also her relationship with the outer objective world. Kip felt a genuine affection for this individual cherry tree, and she was nourished by its sweet fruit for many years. Its death, like the death of her horse J, ripped a piece out of the relational web of her life, which for Kip extends beyond humans to include other creatures. The seemingly bizarre feature of menstrual blood appearing on a tree can be understood as expressing her perception of a real existential connection between two different forms of life, one animal and one plant, joined by their mutual loss of generative powers.

Kip's most ominous environmental dream came later that spring, once the rains had finally stopped and the full scope of the damage became apparent:

> We're going to the beach, except Mother Nature is angry and the tide is dangerously high. A woman is trying to get her baby but as a rescue helicopter gets the child, the woman grabs the helicopter and pulls it to the ground. The waves are massive, coming over the highway. My daughter and I go to an older couple's home before moving on.

She wasn't sure what to make of the woman pulling down the rescue helicopter, though she could definitely relate to the urgent maternal desire to protect one's child. She's had dreams of big waves before, but this time it felt more dangerous, and more personal. In reflecting on the dream, Kip said, "I do think Mother Nature is seriously pissed off at us. We [humans] are like destructive, overpopulating insects." This, I would say, is the mark of a true environmental liberal—humans are no longer the unquestioned masters of nature, but are now called to morally account for their mistreatment of other forms of life.

Border Patrol

In Will's and Kip's dreams we find reflections of the deep ecology perspective that inspires and motivates their political liberalism, and in Sophia's dreams we discover an unusual blending of human-nature kinship with a conservative political outlook. Richard is more typical of conservatives who are not necessarily *anti*environment but who see the relationship between humans and nature very differently from liberals. Instead of mystically merging with nature, Richard and many other conservatives want to preserve a healthy boundary between humans and nature. He recognizes the importance of caring for the natural world and taking responsibility for its well-being, so much so that ten years ago he and his wife started a nonprofit animal rehabilitation clinic in their community, dedicated to treating wild animals who have been found injured or sick.[8] The clinic is run entirely by volunteers, and Richard has devoted countless hours to fund-raising, volunteer recruitment, financial management, and of course treating the animals and trying to ease their suffering. Considering that Richard works a full-time job as a security guard at a local hospital, it's remarkable how dedicated he is to the cause of the animal clinic. Many of his dreams, such as these two, focused directly or indirectly on struggles to keep the clinic going and its stressful impact on his family:

I was in my living room. My daughter and other people were helping me with herding out huge animals. There were cows, hippos, a young elephant, and elk. I know there were other large animals but I don't remember what other kind there were. I remember being concerned that we could be hurt, stepped on, or crushed by them. There was a feeling of fear mixed with confusion, worry, uncertainty, helplessness, and frustration. I also wondered how my wife would deal with this when she got home.

I was handing out forms and trying to get people to take a survey of emotional responses to certain varieties of stimulus. I recall people being skeptical and trying to use my best salesmanlike approach to reassure them. Questions were trying to determine emotions like anger, sensitivity levels, humor, passion, and others... I remember feeling confused and embarrassed when people asked me what this was for, because I didn't know myself.

Richard said the second dream very clearly reflected his waking-world frustrations in trying to persuade people to volunteer for the clinic. He had recently been working hard to recruit new volunteers by distributing flyers, giving public presentations, and making endless phone calls, but he was having little success for his efforts. In the dream, as in waking life, Richard is trying to arouse people's emotions, trying to get them to *feel* for the animals the way he feels for them, but he's finding it's a hard slog. The unwillingness of other people to join him in this mission raises doubts and confusion in his own mind—why exactly is he giving so much of his life to this cause?

It's not because he's a Green. When I asked about the political issues that most concern him, Richard did not list global warming or species extinction among them; he's not that kind of environmentalist. His passionate concern for animal welfare comes from a different psychological source. Rather than surrendering himself *to* nature, Richard is driven to use his personal power for the benefit *of* nature. As we'll see in more detail in the next two chapters, Richard is a tremendously energetic individual whose waking and dreaming life revolves around the themes of power, security, and control. He doesn't question (as deep ecologists do) the dominance of humans over other creatures, but he is sensitive to the harmful effects of human civilization on the wildlife in his area, and he feels a strong ethical responsibility to care for those wounded creatures. This is consistent with his other political views, such as his support for President Bush and the Iraq war. Richard praises the president for being a steady leader who is using American power to protect our country's safety and improve the lives of people in other countries who can benefit from our help. In his community Richard tries to be that kind of a leader—a "compassionate conservative," as it were, doing what he feels is morally right and trying to generate as much public support as he can for his mission.

In a few of Richard's dreams the boundary between animals and people becomes dangerously unstable, and the supremacy of human power is called into question by a threatening force from nature. This was one of his most vivid nightmares from the year of journal keeping:

> I was in a Cadillac convertible, sitting in the back seat behind the driver... My wife and daughter were there. We were driving through some fall woods in a nearby town. I recall crossing over railroad tracks several times. At one point I saw four bear cubs and two adult bears walk to the top of a ravine not very far off to our right. They weren't typical bears for this area, they were grizzly bears. We stopped, and so did the bears. I remember being scared because the bears were looking at us and we were in a stopped and open vehicle. I asked the driver to get us out of there and drive us home. The car wouldn't start. Just then five teenagers on bikes were in the woods surrounding the bears. They began teasing the bears with rubber-band guns. I was in extreme fear for them. The kids were laughing, completely oblivious to the danger they were in. The woods were beautiful, all in golden yellows and browns as the sun lit the forest floor. I was in a helpless panic for the kids and us. I recall yelling at the kids to back away and stop provoking the bears. The Big Bear heard me, stood up and then started walking in our direction. I tried to

urge the driver to start driving the car, but he was gone. I told my family to climb a tree as grizzlies don't climb well. Then I woke in a panic.

The first thing that struck Richard about the dream was that he doesn't drive a Cadillac; in fact, he drives an old Buick. It's a beautiful car in the dream, though, one that Richard wouldn't mind having in waking life. To the extent that cars symbolize personal identity (a belief fervently promoted by car manufacturers), a chauffeur-driven convertible Cadillac indicates wealth, luxury, and high social status—success, in other words, the achievement of the American Dream. Richard doesn't really have a Cadillac, but he's blessed with a wife and child, a successful career, a black belt in karate, and a well-earned reputation as a community leader. If anybody's living a good and virtuous American life, it's Richard. And yet the dream suddenly presents him with a threat that challenges the sufficiency of that kind of life. Richard remembered several other bear dreams he'd experienced, and he commented on this one that "bears seem to be my totem, and they are one of the few animals that scare the hell out of me in real life! Not like a phobia. I just don't want to run into any in the woods. I'm always concerned when I'm in the woods in bear country." It's bad enough when Richard's car won't start, but the provocative behavior of the teenagers turns the dream into a full-fledged nightmare. Richard's waking-life knowledge of nature carries into the dream, as he observes the bears and tries to anticipate their behavior. This is *his* style of environmentalism—respecting the powers of the natural world and intelligently maintaining the boundaries that keep humans safe from those powers. The teens show no such respect for nature, and they foolishly taunt the creatures for their own selfish amusement. The challenge for Richard, and for other pro-environment conservatives of his ilk, is what to do about the social forces represented by the teens—the reckless and immature behavior of a few thoughtless people who put everyone else's lives in danger.

Frightening Changes, Bold Solutions

Richard's wife, Grace, also had a dream that expressed a deepseated anxiety about impending changes in the environment. Grace is a conservative who, like her husband, does not consider environmental issues as one of her top political priorities for the country. We'll discuss her dreams more in the next two chapters, but what's interesting in light of this chapter's themes is her direct sense of being affected by global forces of nature:

> I was at my family's cottage. It was a nice sunny day. Everything seemed regular, except the water. The beach was normal, but it seemed to end at the water's edge sharply. The water looked like it was in a huge holding tank—like the lake was in an in-ground pool. I noticed it right away and didn't understand why. It concerned me and I felt the world was changing and it might not be for the good. I tried to relax a bit, but seemed to know (in my dream) that a change in the world would be taking place in the not too distant future.

Grace spent the happiest days of her childhood at her family's vacation cottage, where she swam, boated, and fished all summer long. More perhaps than anyone else in the dreamers' focus group, Grace's life revolves around the people in her family, and she's especially sensitive to anything that can be perceived as a threat to them. The scenario portrayed by her dream isn't very severe as environmental changes go—just a new and more formally divided separation between natural and human realms—

but what stands out is her strange, unshakable feeling that worse developments are yet to come. This small but worrisome change at the physical and emotional center of her family's experience with nature strikes her as an ill omen for the future.

It would be untrue to say that Grace's attitude toward environmental issues completely changed because of this dream. The impact of single dreams on waking behavior is rarely that simple. But what Grace's dream does suggest is that she is open to an environmentalist appeal that focuses on her overriding concern for the well-being of her family. As will become clearer in the coming chapters, Grace is most attracted to politicians whose primary goals are to provide the basic conditions necessary for a healthy continuation of American family traditions. If she were persuaded that those traditions were truly in imminent danger because of damage to the environment, she would very likely become an enthusiastic supporter of governmental efforts to protect against that danger.

We turn for a final word on the subject to Dan, who would probably count as the most traditionally conservative person in the group in relation to environmental issues. A mystical feeling of union with nature (of Will's or Kip's variety, at least) is not part of his spiritual path. He enjoys the eminently nonliberal sports of hunting and fishing, and he does not favor adding new laws to protect the environment. Rather, he wants "more enforcement of current laws." Other than two brief incidents of fishing, the only animal to appear in his dreams was the malevolent snake we discussed in chapter 2. All in all, Dan seems the least likely person to advocate radical alterations in the way Americans relate to the environment and use natural resources. Yet that's exactly what he did when I asked him what he would do if he had the power to make one change in America to improve the country's hopes for the future: "Reduce dependency on oil. This would make our country a more peaceful place because oil influences politics. There would be less need to protect oil fields in other countries. The more protection they need, the more influence we have on these foreign countries. This change would lessen our political and physical influences/dependency toward other countries, which create hostility and other problems. Also, this change would create a cleaner environment."

If anyone knows from personal experience the destructive consequences of America's "addiction to oil" (President Bush's words), it's Dan. His commonsense argument is consistent with the way he approaches other situations in life—identify potential dangers and take decisive action to protect against them. Too much demand for oil is harming American interests and threatening our national security, upon which everything else depends. We have it within our power to cut domestic oil consumption, and we should do so because it would improve our country's safety, with the added benefit of a less polluted environment.

Sounds like a solid conservative argument, doesn't it? But of course Dan's proposal runs counter to the policy positions of the Republicans he usually supports. It's hard to know how many other conservatives are like Dan, committed to the Republicans yet favoring much more forceful changes to energy policy than the party's leaders have been willing to make. I suspect he's not alone, and he may in fact represent a large portion of the American public—people who are willing to make dramatic adjustments in energy usage in order to protect the country's long-term welfare. Environmental issues as defined by most liberals do not factor into these people's concerns. But as Dan acknowledges, the policy changes they want to make would have environmental benefits just as real as if they were motivated by a deep ecology perspective.

Shamanic Knowledge

The idea that dreaming provides an experiential source of nature wisdom goes farther back than Emerson, Thoreau, and the New England transcendentalists. It goes back farther even than the dream-saturated cultures (collectively known as Native Americans) that peopled this continent for thousands of years before the arrival of European colonists. Those cultures are themselves descendents of Neolithic-era humans in Asia who migrated across the Bering Strait land bridge some ten thousand years ago. Earlier than that, our historical vision becomes cloudy. But we have good evidence to believe that those Neolithic communities regarded dreaming as a powerful means of connection with the forces of nature.[9] Many of these communities had ritual specialists (known in Siberia as *shamans*) whose extraordinary skill at dream exploration enhanced their ecological knowledge, healing power, and divinatory insight. Shamans served as mediators between humans and the greater forces of nature, defending their communities against danger and promoting the group's welfare and prosperity.

The point in bringing this up is to highlight the deep historical roots of our dreaming engagement with the environment. As far back in time as we can see, humans have looked to their dreams for help with communal challenges, particularly when those challenges involve dangerous interactions with the powers of nature. Of course, Americans today live in radically different circumstances from those earlier human groups—we get our food by driving to the grocery store, not by hunting wild animals. *But we still dream.* Just like our cave-dwelling ancestors, we enter each night into a different state of consciousness in which the ordinary boundaries of life become porous and fluid, where the waking ego yields to the spontaneous visions of the creative imagination.

In that liminal, betwixt-and-between space, the sharp separation of modern humans from their natural surroundings dissolves, and a new kind of relationship with the environment becomes possible. Nature stops being an "it"; we begin to see ourselves as elements in a larger ecological whole. That's the crucial first step toward a more responsible approach to the politics of environmental protection.

5

Work and Money

When James Truslow Adams first spoke of "the American Dream," he tried to distinguish its pursuit from simple money-making. The founding vision of our country, he claimed, "has not been a dream of merely material plenty."[1] Still, Adams had to acknowledge that a big part of America's appeal has always been the lure of wealth and the opportunity to improve one's financial well-being. The country's historical preference for a loosely regulated market economy has allowed people from many different backgrounds to envision and create successful businesses that have made them rich, or at least elevated their economic fortunes far above where they started. What Tocqueville saw as the plodding industriousness of American life has been experienced by millions of people as something much more noble and uplifting. In working hard and striving to improve their economic lot, Americans have found a deeply fulfilling way of developing their mental and physical abilities and increasing their prospects for more growth and prosperity in the future.

In present-day America the most widely accepted sign that a person has achieved the dream is owning a home. The U.S. government has many policies in place to encourage and support home ownership, and politicians of both major parties regularly justify their initiatives as promoting people's financial ability to buy a house. Several classic American values are bundled together in this potent symbol, including the need for personal security, the pleasure of owning and controlling a piece of nature, the yearning to be free from external constraints, and the desire to protect and nurture one's family. Indeed, I suspect the symbol's allure is partly responsible for the home mortgage crisis of the past couple of years. Many of the people caught up in the financial firestorm of foreclosures and bankruptcies were first-time buyers whose eagerness to actualize the American Dream clouded their judgment about their financial ability to meet the terms of their mortgages.

Fortunately, none of the focus group members has gone through financial difficulties this dire. Almost all of them, however, feel uncomfortably close to the economic edge. Anxieties about work, money, and financial security weigh heavily on their minds, in their waking lives and in their dreams. One of the most common themes across all their dream journals was workplace frustration, which accurately reflected their bleak waking-life attitudes about their current jobs. To listen to this group of people, Americans are incredibly stressed by their work, far beyond what is healthy or humane. As their dreams reveal, both liberals and conservatives want much more attention to issues of economic fairness and dignity in the workplace. They are literally sick of working as hard as they do, and they're angry at the social and economic elites who manipulate the country's financial system for their own personal enrichment.

Entering the Workforce

The reason we haven't heard much from Nadine, the twenty-four-year-old living in Florida, is that she had to drop out of the group after five months of intermittent journal keeping. She started the project with great enthusiasm and expected it to be fairly easy since she usually had no trouble remembering her dreams. But once the journal-keeping year began, she found the stress of working two jobs (as a landscaper during the day and a waitress at night) was making it impossible to continue the journaling with any regularity. "My work hours screw up my sleep patterns," she said. Combined with the emotional challenges of preparing for her wedding and helping her fiancé mourn the death of his mother, Nadine hit a point where she couldn't handle any extra responsibilities, even for something she would under most circumstances enjoy doing.

I find it telling that the two members of the group whose work lives most directly interfered with their journal keeping were a soldier and a waitress. Not to demean the uniquely stressful conditions of combat, but anyone who's worked in a restaurant knows the physical intensity, long hours, and emotional self-control required of the waitstaff. These kinds of working conditions make it almost impossible to maintain a steady, healthful pattern of sleep. This came out in the very first dream Nadine recorded in her journal:

> I was on an island with hundreds of people, at some kind of resort. I worked there, so I had access to the employee quarters. I worked there but I didn't fit in with everyone else. After work everyone would get all dressed up really racy, like they were going to a club, and all the employees would become escorts of sorts. I remember wanting to run away.

She had been working in restaurants for the past three years, trying to save up money to buy a home with her soon-to-be husband. Someday she hoped to finish her college degree, but for now her focus was on achieving financial independence. Nadine was acutely conscious of the fact that most of the people she worked with at the restaurant were like the people in the dream, "just a mass of followers with their own agendas who sell themselves for money, a good time, a good feeling." She struggled to maintain her own goals and resist the temptation to fall into those kinds of habits: "I feel that I am different—or maybe I could have the potential to be like them, but I don't want to be."

The psychological strain of this effort can be clearly seen in her sleep and dream experiences. Of the sixty-eight nights she made an entry in her journal, Nadine says she slept well only seven times. She reported thirty-nine nights of fair sleep and twenty-one nights of poor sleep.[2] That's by far the worst self-rated sleep quality of any of the ten participants and an ominous sign for Nadine's long-term physical and emotional welfare. She reported a total of thirty-six dreams, for a recall rate of about one dream every other night. This is at the high end of the recall scale, consistent with Nadine's young age and personal history of interest in dreaming. Most of her dreams were long (requiring more than two hundred words to report), extraordinarily imaginative (two-thirds were bizarre, only one-third mundane), and very negative (almost half were full-blown nightmares). These patterns match what we found in the poll regarding the propensity of young, liberal women to experience poor sleep and troubling dreams. Nadine locates herself on the leftward side of the political spectrum—"I guess I'm closer to liberal"—mostly because she's in favor of same-sex marriage, abortion rights, and alternative approaches to spirituality. But the political issue she identified as her number-one concern was affirmative action. She strongly opposes it because she thinks it distorts the awarding of financial aid for college tuition (Nadine had to drop out of college because she couldn't get enough loan money to continue). So there's a conservative streak to her still-emerging political identity that focuses on her perceptions of economic fairness. She wants to stay true to her deeper inclinations to be spiritually open and culturally tolerant, but the financial pressures of her life are generating a crosscurrent of populist indignation against the usual liberal positions on affirmative action, welfare, and immigration. She's feeling under attack in her day-to-day existence (her nightmares are not only frequent but unusually intense and violent), and in political terms she's very receptive to arguments for more justice and equality in the government's treatment of ordinary, hardworking citizens.

The Daily Grind

I could easily fill a whole book with nothing but people's nightmares about work. For the average American, this seems to be the most common type of dream experience. Forget about dreams of flying, losing your teeth, being naked in public—those are dramatic when they happen, but in terms of actual frequency they're extremely rare. If you look at people's experiences on a nightly basis across a long stretch of time, you're going to find many of them dreaming about problems at work far more than any other subject. Every occupation has its distinctive nightmare scenario —a doctor losing a patient, a truck driver getting in an accident, a newscaster unable to speak, a student late or unprepared for a test. And just as people continue to suffer late-for-exam dreams long after their student days are past, they frequently have work nightmares many years after they've left a previous job, sometimes with weird metamorphoses of one bad job situation into another. In the first month of keeping her journal Kip, the California rancher, had one of these latter experiences:

> Waitress nightmare dream. I am at the ranch, only it's not the same, and I am feeding the horses. There are more and more of them in odd places, then there are people to serve

115

breakfast to. There are hundreds of them. All need to be served eggs sunny-side up. They are everywhere. I can't possibly do it all. I hate giving "bad service." A guy I know is in the dream. I am relying on him to bring hay, but he is unreliable. I haven't got enough of anything to take care of all these people and horses. There are lots of hills. I seem to be always walking uphill.

The last time Kip worked as a waitress was more than twenty years ago, yet here she is in the familiar nightmare scenario of "too many customers to serve," a recurrent dream that merges with similarly helpless feelings generated by her current work 'situation at the ranch. She saw the connection right away: "The ranch is often overwhelming to care for—it has been lately." She associated the detail about the eggs to her depressed feeling that "sometimes it's really difficult to put on a 'sunny-side up' attitude." And the hilly terrain may be unrealistic in regards to the physical landscape of the ranch, but it's intuitively true as a metaphorical image of her psychological landscape: "The hills— I feel I am struggling up a hill all the time. Everything is hard to keep together—finances, fences, A-Z."

Making a living as a ranch manager in twenty-first-century America is no easy chore. Kip isn't looking for direct governmental support so much as a fundamental change in the way everyone treats each other socially and economically. The hardest part of her job isn't the physical labor, as exhausting as that can be. No, what really gets Kip down is other people's failure to do their fair share of the necessary work. Her sadness and frustration are rooted in her deep ecology belief in the connection among all forms of life. She doesn't understand why people don't recognize their moral obligations as members of an interdependent community. Just as she sees humans failing to act responsibly at a global level ("we are sort of a plague on the planet"), every day

Kip sees people at the ranch (like the guy in her dream) who are failing to act responsibly at the local, interpersonal level. These kinds of negative emotions and unpleasant interactions from the workplace filter into her dreams, and they cast a shadow over her political attitudes in waking life, too. Kip is sharply and defiantly liberal in almost every area of domestic and foreign policy, and yet her dark view of human nature resonates more with the conservative caution of Edmund Burke than the liberal optimism of Rousseau and Locke. Kip doubts that human beings will ever rise above their primal selfishness and fear of others, and she holds only faint hopes for any meaningful change in America's future.

Still, she's committed to doing the right thing herself, and that means participating in the electoral process. Looking at the early stages of the 2008 presidential race, she said she was attracted by the freshness of Barack Obama's campaign and its promise of smart and honest leadership. She said Obama shares many of the best qualities found in the politician she most admires: Ann Richards. Kip was very sad when the eloquent, quick-witted former Texas governor died during the journal-keeping year, and she wishes someone like Richards would appear to restore her kind of earthy wisdom and populist good sense to the American political system.

Grace, the preschool teacher from New York, comes from an entirely different work life and family situation, but she shares with Kip many of the same personal frustrations and economic anxieties. Grace and her husband, Richard, endured some tight financial times during the journal-keeping year, and midway through she decided she needed to take a second job. While she and Richard were considering her best options in this depressing situation, she had the following dream:

> I remember being in a very crowded grocery store. It wasn't a large store, but I realized I was working there.

There were tons of people waiting in line to check out. Everyone in line was looking at me—hoping I could help out. The clerk yelled to me—"Get some other checkout people." I said, "OK, I'll be right back!" The next thing I knew was that I was in some other room stacking wooden boxes. I was soon being creative and making some art form with the wooden boxes. I made a really cool arch *[she drew a picture of it in her journal]*. It looked really attractive. Someone came up to it and knocked it over, not sure if it was intentional or not. Then I woke up.

She knew that finding a retail job at some place like a grocery store would be the quickest and easiest way to supplement the family income. But she really didn't want to go that route, and her dream confirmed her deep-seated feelings of resistance. Life was already hard enough, and Grace wanted to avoid a second job that would thrust her into this kind of retail nightmare scenario where personal creativity counted for so little.

Alas, after two months of searching, Grace realized she didn't have any better options. So she went ahead and took a position as cashier at a local supermarket, working the overnight shift. The extra income definitely helped with the financial crunch, but it threw her sleep cycle completely out of whack, and its emotional cost was severe in terms of how she felt about her family:

I was at work. I saw my mother approaching in my direction. I thought, "What is she doing here?" When she came closer, she told me that my aunt, uncle, and cousins were also with her and they came to visit me. I told her that I really couldn't visit with everyone at work. My mom then told me that we would all meet up during my lunch. Soon I was at my mom's house visiting with my relatives. In my head I was thinking, "I can't believe I came here during my very short lunch time." The rest of the dream consisted of me trying to get back to work, with many things stopping me or holding me up. I couldn't find the right school bus to put my daughter on, I couldn't find transportation. Once I got to work, I couldn't seem to find my way to where I was supposed to be. The whole dream was total frustration.

For someone like Grace, who values family above all else, the conflict could not be more sharply drawn. Worries about money were directly impacting her ability to care for her daughter and stay connected with her extended family. She had to take the second job to preserve her family's well-being, and yet when she worked she had to separate herself both physically and emotionally from her family. She's doing her best, but it never seems to be enough.

Grace has little use for Republican *or* Democratic leaders who promise to improve the economic situation of middle-class Americans. "I hate politics!" she said with great gusto when I first asked her about her political views. She's fed up with all the negativity she sees on TV and hears on the radio, and she deliberately tries to pay as little attention as she can to the daily news. She doesn't feel good about avoiding current events ("Maybe that's bad..."), but in her present circumstances it's one of the few ways she can control and protect her emotional balance.

Balance is exactly what she loses in the following dream, which came at a particularly low point in their family financial situation, when much depended on the quick arrival of Richard's most recent paycheck:

My husband and I were walking into my husband's workplace. For some reason we had to take a narrow concrete

119

bridge to get inside. The bridge was only about a foot wide and was way high up off the ground. As we walked, the concrete on the left side crumbled and fell off the bridge. In a quick response, I threw myself toward the right and held on for dear life. I told my husband to do the same. Although the bridge was very high, we seemed to be very close to the ceiling of the place. As I held onto the side, I looked at the rest of the concrete to see if it was cracking, too. I said, "We have to hurry and get off of this!" Since we were now very close to the ceiling, I crawled forward. There was no opening to get into the building. I searched with my eyes quickly in every direction. Then I thought, "This is a dream, I can get out of this." The next thing I knew—my husband and I were walking up a few stairs and entering a building.

As in Kip's dream of the distorted ranch/restaurant where everything is uphill, Grace finds her financial troubles portrayed as nightmarish threats of falling, collapse, and being squeezed in a tight place. It may be just a stray detail that the bridge crumbles on the left and Grace instinctively jumps for safety to the right. Then again, it may also be an accurate metaphor of her shifting political beliefs, which Grace says (when she can stand to talk about politics at all) are gradually moving from a liberal to a more conservative point of view. In this dream she certainly displays the quality of personal initiative that conservatives value so much. The experience of becoming lucid or self-aware in a dream occurs very rarely for most people, but when it does it's often during a nightmare. Just at the moment of greatest fear, when all seems lost and one's doom seems assured, the cavalry of rational consciousness rides to the rescue of the helpless dreaming self. In a previous research study I found this kind of experience (i.e., the appearance of lucidity enabling the dreamer to escape and/or control the dream itself) occurring more frequently among conservatives than liberals.[3] Grace's case seems to reflect a similar kind of dynamic. She's relying almost exclusively on her own personal resources to face her fears and establish a stable and realistic attitude toward life's difficulties. When she started her new job at the market and found herself immediately swamped with complicated tasks, she turned to the practice of repeating "positive affirmations" such as, *I can do this with no problem and I will enjoy it.* She's holding on as best she can, just like in her dream, hoping for the psychological control and spiritual strength she needs to keep herself and her family together.

Made in America

As much as they dislike their jobs and worry about their family finances, many if not most Americans still take pride in their work and consider it an opportunity to express their best talents and creative energies. Richard is a good example of this. In his job as a security guard, in his volunteer leadership of the animal clinic, and in his martial arts practices, Richard throws himself into his work, dedicating himself to high standards of efficiency, usefulness, and self-control. Like Grace, he feels burdened by their constant money troubles, and he bitterly resents the poor treatment he and other employees receive at the hospital where he works. A quite bizarre dream Richard reported about a week after starting the journal highlighted his unhappy feelings about his job:

> I was standing in our cafeteria's cash register line at work.
> The next thing I knew, the line became an obstacle course
> to get to your food. I was up on a roof of a tall building,
> trying to walk across a plank bridging two roofs. On the

roof across on the other side were two halves of a tuna sub sandwich I ordered. As I was about to step onto the plank, an earthquake shook and my bridge fell. Roofs and build-ings everywhere were in various states of ruin. People were scrambling about everywhere! Some were in fear, while others were angry that they couldn't get to their food. People were fighting over food that others had.

The resemblance to his wife's dream of a crumbling bridge is probably not a coincidence. Married couples and family mem-bers occasionally dream of the same themes and images, a phenomenon that naturally arises in conditions of emotional in-timacy and shared living. There's nothing paranormal about this —it's just one of the ways that dreaming reflects whatever's most important in a person's waking life. For both Richard and Grace, financial anxieties topped the list, and their shared dream of a falling bridge metaphorically expressed their feelings of eco-nomic insecurity. Richard said the dream was directly referring to the fact that the hospital has cut multiple staff positions over the past few years, putting greater strains on those employees still remaining. According to Richard, one of the most frustrating consequences of these job changes is that "the cafeteria lines and wait at the register have been long, reducing by half our thirty-minute lunch period." This might sound like a minor complaint, but for working people like Richard their lunch break is the only time they have that belongs entirely to them, when they can eat, socialize, and relax in freedom from their employers' demands. To disrupt that precious time without any concern for the psy-chological impact on the employees is to invite a sharp rise in their anger and alienation.

Richard's sympathy for his wife's job difficulties appears in this dream, which occurred a couple of months after she'd begun working at the supermarket:

In this dream I was just hired as the store manager for our local Wal-Mart. I recall trying to count the revenue to prepare it for the bank. Each time I got part of the way into counting, I would be interrupted, lose count, and have to start over. Once, after resuming my counting, I had trouble focusing and seemed to forget how to count. The final time my parents (including my father, who is dead) came into the store. They invited me to have dinner at a restaurant. I simply set the piles of money on some boxes in plain view of shoppers in a store aisle and left with my parents. In the restaurant I realized that I left the store revenue unsecured. I felt panic and went back to the store. I was very worried that I would be fired. When I got back to the store, the piles of money were still sitting where I left them, with a note from the district manager saying he wanted to see me in the office. The manager told me that a customer reported the money just sitting on the box. He said he wasn't going to fire me because the money was still there, but I had to suffer the consequences.

Very much as in Grace's nightmare of retail overload, Richard finds himself torn in a dream between his job responsibilities and his desire to spend time with his parents. His father (who died a couple years earlier) appeared in several of Richard's dreams during the year of journal keeping, mostly in friendly, happy contexts. His appearance in this dream created a painful conflict for Richard, forcing him to confront two seemingly incompatible desires.

It's notable that Richard has trouble counting in the dream, because recent evidence from neuroscience indicates that during REM sleep (the time when most but not all dreaming occurs) the brain's ability to perform linear reasoning tasks like solving math problems and calculating finances is greatly diminished.[4]

The intrusion of that kind of mental activity into dreaming is bound to be difficult and frustrating, and yet it's almost impossible to avoid for people like Richard who are dealing with relentless money problems in their waking lives. He said, "I think this dream was made up of listening to stories from my wife about her new job, and a combination of hating my job and being frustrated that I can't seem to catch up on all the things I have to do in my life."

His recurrent bear dreams factor in here, too. He had a particularly vivid one a couple of nights before the 2006 elections in which weirdly growling bears were approaching from the woods around his animal clinic. The dream frightened him so much he awoke in a full-body panic. The intensity of the emotion seems to have triggered a kind of "Aha!" moment of insight, as he wrote following the dream:

> I think I've finally realized [the meaning of] the bear in all my dreams. It evokes such a fear in me that I now believe it means something I have or feel I have no control over. Lately I've felt very bad that Grace has to work a second part-time job so we can stay ahead of our bills. This is something I feel powerless to change. It's larger than my abilities, and scares me. Our financial situation seems to be out of my control at the moment, making me feel like I'm at fault, not able to do enough to support us on just my salary alone, and having to watch my wife work physically harder than she should. This is my bear: I can't control it, and it scares the hell out of me.

His realization turns on the two meanings of the word *bear:* as a large, dangerous animal and as a verb meaning to carry a burden. Richard can't stop the bears in his dreams, and he can't bear to watch his wife work so hard in waking life. The pun-mediated fusion of these profound fears generates his worst recurrent nightmare.

Richard still has his pride in a job well done, and he works very hard to be of help to others. Midway through the journal-keeping year he won an award at the hospital for his outstanding service "above and beyond the call of duty" when he spent several days translating for a very sick patient who was deaf (Richard is fluent in American Sign Language). This experience prompted a bizarre but telling dream:

> I was in Iraq helping the government as an interpreter. For whatever reason, it seems I had the unique ability to utter any nonsense, and the Iraqi people could understand me. Even though I can't speak a word of any Middle Eastern language, just by faking it, they all knew what I meant. People were amazed at my ability.

At one level, Richard's dream is a silly bit of fantasy. But at another level it's a nice example of how the imaginings of our sleeping minds can reveal the powerful wishes that inspire our views of the world. Richard's desire to work on behalf of a higher cause comes through clearly here—he wants a challenge that's worthy of his intense devotion and heroic energy, a challenge that's metaphorically equivalent to serving the country in wartime. As mentioned in chapter 3, Richard said he would enlist in the military right now if he were young enough to do so. He's familiar with news reports about our government's lack of Arabic-speaking translators, and his dream accurately identifies an area in which the U.S. military needs help. The fact that he doesn't really speak Arabic is finessed by his strangely nonverbal, glossolalia-like utterances that somehow do the trick of establishing a communications link between the Americans and the Iraqis. Richard's dream leaves him with the tantalizing feeling that he possesses inner powers capable of helping him achieve the success he so fervently desires, building bridges rather than falling off them. This, I suggest, is the true faith of a political conservative: the trust in one's own deep personal wellspring of moral virtue and autonomous willpower. Richard expects America's leaders to share his supreme faith in the individual, and he'll remain a committed Republican as long as the party continues to champion this central ideal of heroic self-reliance.

No Time for Dreaming

Pulling back from the fine details of the dream journals to the broader picture provided by the sleep and dream poll, we find additional insight into the psychological conditions of American workers, particularly at the opposite ends of the income scale. According to this poll, people who earn less than $30,000 a year are much more likely to sleep six or fewer hours a night as compared to people who earn $100,000 or more. Poor Americans are twice as likely as the wealthy to have multiple nights of troubled sleep.

Income and Sleep Patterns

Sleep patterns		Less than $30K (%)	More than $100K (%)
Duration	Fewer than 6 hours a night	24	6
	6–8.9 hours a night	70	91
	9 or more hours a night	5	3
Insomnia	Never	50	63
	1–2 nights a week	20	21
	3 or more nights a week	29	14

The conclusion here is entirely unsurprising: rich people in America sleep better, and poor people sleep worse. How could it be otherwise? Rich people usually have a high degree of both economic and social power; they're more in control of their lives, and they enjoy more opportunities for leisure and rest. Poor people by definition lack economic and social power, and their day-to-day lives are more vulnerable to external threats and unexpected changes. These pressures evidently impact them at night, too, in the form of diminished amounts of sleep and disrupted quality of their rest.

All the responses to the dream questions reveal a slight but marked advantage for the wealthier people.

Income and Dream Patterns

Dream type	Less than $30K (%)	More than $100K (%)
A person who's now dead appearing alive	39	40
Magically flying in the air	21	26
Being chased or attacked	40	49
Falling	47	52
Sexual experiences	40	50
Being in a situation exactly like your regular waking life	53	59
Being aware you're dreaming and able to control the dream	36	51

The biggest difference was on the last question, about having control within the dream state. That makes sense in relation to the respondents' power differences in waking life. The higher rate of flying and sexual dreams of the wealthy also suggests greater degrees of power and pleasure. However, the wealthy also have more nightmarish dreams of falling and being chased. Perhaps this reflects their fears of losing the privilege and security of their high social status; perhaps it reflects an overall expansion of dreaming experience among those with greater financial security. Thus another fault line in American dreaming opens along the familiar divisions of economic class. Those who are at the low end of the American income scale are also at the low end of the sleeping and dreaming scale. Those who enjoy economic abundance in their waking lives also enjoy psychological abundance in their sleeping and dreaming.

This brings us back to Adams and his conviction that the American Dream is not simply about making money and getting rich, but about our higher aspiration for creative freedom and personal independence. Most Americans believe that's true. But it's also true that not having enough money makes it harder to sleep and dream. Not having enough money makes *everything* harder, of course. But not getting enough sleep is an especially harmful consequence of poverty because sleep deprivation (as we've already noted) diminishes a person's physical, intellectual, and emotional abilities, making it significantly harder for the individual to function well in his or her waking life. The narrower range of dreaming among low-income people also seems to be a reflection of their limited sphere of control and power in waking life. They're farthest away from the American Dream, and farthest from a healthy connection with their personal sleeping and dreaming.

Worst of all from any perspective is being homeless, which the federal government defines as the condition of a person without a regular, normal place to sleep. The McKinney-Vento Homeless Assistance Act of 1987 defines a homeless person as:

(1) an individual who lacks a fixed, regular, and adequate nighttime residence; and (2) an individual who has a pri-

mary nighttime residence that is—(A) a supervised publicly or privately operated shelter designed to provide temporary living accommodations (including welfare hotels,
congregate shelters, and transitional housing for the mentally ill); (B) an institution that provides a temporary residence for persons intended to be institutionalized; or (C) a
public or private place not designed for, or ordinarily used
as, a regular sleeping accommodation for human beings.

Homeless people are those whose economic fortunes are so
bad that they do not have a safe and secure place to rest at night.[5]
Some of them sleep in crowded, dangerous shelters; others sleep
on the streets, exposed to the elements; still others avoid sleep as
much as they can, afraid of being attacked. Again, given what we
know about the negative effects of sleep deprivation, it's hard to
imagine how these sleep-starved people will ever be able to rally
the physical and psychological strength necessary to find a steady
and self-sufficient place in the American economy.

Populist Rumblings from the Psychic Depths

We've now considered several stories of people from different
political perspectives who share similarly intense degrees of frustration and dissatisfaction with their jobs. What's remarkable isn't
just the high proportion of overstressed, poorly treated workers
in the United States. Rather, it's the fact that these people don't
have a more effective voice in American politics. The Democrats
present themselves as the strongest advocates for economic equality and worker rights (presidential candidate John Edwards has
pushed hardest in this direction), but that hasn't impressed
Richard, Grace, Dan, or other conservatives who believe a liberal government would probably just change the current unfair
system into something even worse. The Republican Party at-
tracts these people because of its emphasis on personal virtue as the

basis for a successful economic life in America. However, while Republicans sing the praises of the free market, they tend to downplay the physical and emotional impact of real-world economic hardship on the less privileged members of society. The pervasive feelings of anger, anxiety, and distress among American workers are thus diffused across both political parties, draining away the collective energy that would be necessary to effect meaningful change.

6

Family Values

Sooner or later, anyone who studies dreams must confront the ghost of Sigmund Freud. For the past hundred years his ideas have dominated Western attitudes toward dreaming among both scientists and the general public. Yet Freud's psychoanalytic theory has turned out to be badly mistaken about many aspects of human psychology, and if he tried to use his bullying methods of psychotherapy with patients today, he'd probably land in jail for malpractice. I've emphasized several times that my approach to dreams does not depend on his outdated theory or questionable methods of interpretation. That being said, I also believe Freud was right about a few things. He was right that dreams are meaningful expressions of people's wishes, fears, and conflicts. He was right that people often avoid facing unpleasant truths about themselves. And he was right that our family relationships have a profound impact on our psychological development and growth, not only in early childhood but all through our lives. Freud may not have been the first person to claim any of this, but he expressed these psychological insights in eloquent and thought-provoking terms, and those of us in the field of dream research will always be indebted to him.

In *The Interpretation of Dreams* (1900), his first and arguably greatest book, Freud focused much of his attention on dreams as revelations of people's unconscious feelings about their families. Some of these revelations were dark and frightening (e.g., wishing a sibling would die, feeling sexual desire for a parent), and Freud believed the repression of those desires was the ultimate cause of his patients' psychosomatic sufferings. The main weakness of psychoanalytic dream theory stems from Freud's assumption that his patients (mostly young women from well-to-do Jewish families living in late nineteenth-/early twentieth-century Vienna) were representative of all humans in all places and times. If we broaden our research lens and look at the dreams of a wider variety of individuals (e.g., people other than psychiatric patients), we find that these kinds of "family drama" dreams are actually quite rare, even accounting for the factors of resistance and repression. The oedipal complex is not, as Freud claimed, the key to all dream interpretation. Nevertheless, the psychoanalytic emphasis on family dynamics in dreaming remains useful. In the present book we've considered several dreams in which family members, both living and dead, interact with the dreamer in meaningful and emotionally impactful ways. Here is another place where patterns of dreaming can reveal people's highest ideals and most important values (along with their worst fears and most painful conflicts).

This opens up a new opportunity to study the political psychology of conservatives and liberals, because fierce debates over "family values" have played a prominent role in American politics for many years. In election after election sharp disagreements have erupted over issues of sexual morality, reproductive rights, cultural decency, educational methods, adoption policies, and the definition of marriage. Both parties justify virtually everything they do as service to the cause of America's families, and they regularly attack each other for alleged crimes against the family. Knowing a bit about Freud and psychoanalysis helps us understand why these issues are so emotionally arousing and prone to spark political conflict. In this chapter we'll take a final look at the dream journals of the focus group to see how their family interactions in dreaming correlate with their political beliefs about issues of sex, morality, and culture.

Threats to the Family

Let's start with the fact that all members of the group recorded at least a few dreams involving threats or dangers to their families. Some people (Nadine, Sophia, Elizabeth, Kip) had multiple nightmares of attacks, accidents, illnesses, and losses befalling members of their family. The frequency of these anxiety-provoking dreams makes sense not only in terms of Freudian psychoanalysis but also in light of recent developments in evolutionary psychology. If it's true, as evolutionary psychologists claim, that the human mind is cognitively designed with a special set of abilities (language, empathy, face recognition, episodic memory, etc.) enabling one to survive in a small, family-based social group like the tribes and clans of our earliest ancestors, then we would expect to find some indication of these social reasoning abilities in people's dreams, too. And we do find them, in abundance. Dreams of family danger stand out because their intense emotionality makes them highly memorable and impactful on the individual's waking life. The psychological potency of these nightmares seems to be rooted in the natural fear common to all humans of losing our kin—that is, losing vital pieces of the interpersonal network that makes our individual lives possible.

We've already had the chance to look at Grace's dreams as reflections of her views of work and nature. Now we can turn to her family dreams, which so clearly mirror the importance in waking life of her husband, daughter, parents, siblings, and other relatives. It helps in understanding Grace's view of life to know that early in her marriage she and Richard had fertility problems preventing them from conceiving their own biological children. This situation put enormous emotional strain on both of them, and Grace says at one point she broke down and prayed to God to help her find a solution. Soon after that, they adopted a baby girl whom they've raised as their daughter ever since. It's clear in talking with Grace that she appreciates, perhaps more than most people, the joy of raising a child and the satisfaction of contributing to her family's growth and prosperity. Looking at her dreams, we find more than half of them include a family member, a remarkably high percentage and the most of anyone in the group. In many of these dreams she's in a position of trying to help, protect, or care for a family member in need. Threats, dangers, problems, and hassles come from all directions, and some of her dreams turn into overwhelming nightmares. But significantly, most of them don't. Grace's dreaming self usually finds a way to deal with the threatening situation, either through her own personal effort or by means of external aid. She possesses a great deal of inner strength that seems capable of modulating (if not entirely eliminating) the negativity appearing at the outset of many of her dream experiences. Here's a dream she had early in the journal-keeping year, when the financial pressures on her and Richard were starting to build:

> I was driving in my car, my husband and daughter were with me. As I drove up a very steep roadway, I noticed the truck in front of me was losing his load of bricks. They were all tumbling out as he started to go over the top of the hill. I quickly hit my brakes and told the others to brace themselves and expect a lot of noise as the bricks hit

our car and go under it. Soon the bricks were avalanching down the hill quickly toward us. I continued to press hard on the brake. The bricks were soon all around us, but not one hit the car. They all slid alongside the car or underneath without one hit. My husband turned around to look and remarked how incredible it was that we were not touched. As I looked behind our car, I noticed the other cars and trucks were caught up in the brick avalanche and were rolling and crashing down the hill behind us. I said, "It must be because I put my brakes on right away and maybe they didn't." We didn't know the reason, but were quite relieved.

The phrase "hit like a ton of bricks" comes to mind with this dream, which Grace said definitely felt like an accurate portrayal of her economic anxieties at that time: she's doing her best to protect her family from dangerous, uncontrollable forces crashing down from the outside world. She relies as much as possible on her own strength and resourcefulness, but she's also aware that benevolent and even miraculous forces are active in her life as well. Grace is a deeply spiritual person who knows from personal experience the power of prayer, and she firmly believes the very existence of her family is a blessing from God. The nightmarish elements of the dream (an avalanche of bricks) honestly reflect the real dangers facing her family, and her quick response to the danger (slamming on the brakes) shows her willingness to take personal action to protect her family. She knows, however, both in the dream and in waking life, that her own efforts will never be enough. The miraculous element in the dream (being untouched by the avalanche) reassures her that she's not alone, that some being or principle of divine goodness is guarding her daughter, her husband, and herself.

The dream Grace reported right before this one centered on a happy, extremely vivid, and highly memorable encounter with her deceased father:

> I was in my mother's house. She was in the kitchen. I was in the dining room and was checking for water leaks at the outside wall. I felt tiny splashes of water on my face, and I said, "I think you have a leak." I noticed someone in the living room. I turned to look, and my father was sitting on the couch, smiling. He was acting like "Surprise!" I ran over to see him, it was sooo real. I said that it was so nice to see him again. He looked very well. He was wearing a very bright royal blue dress shirt. It was not something that he would normally wear. The buttons up the front and on his cuffs were pearl white. I wanted to hug him, but didn't because I normally did not do that when he was alive. He was very cheerful and gave a quick explanation why there was water in the dining room. I don't remember what he said about the water, though.

Grace and Richard both take keen interest in these dreams, considering them real encounters with the spirits of their deceased loved ones. Grace said, "This dream stayed with me all day." The positive feelings from this visitation experience reflect Grace's sense of transcendent family powers looking out for her well-being. In this way her beliefs about her family are woven directly into her spiritual beliefs and practices. In addition to divine guidance and personal effort, Grace also relied on Richard to help in protecting the family. The fear that he might fail comes out in this false-awakening, home-invasion nightmare:

> The first part started with finding my daughter's bike outside. I guess she did not put it in the garage at night.

Someone took it all apart and left only the frame. The bike was small and light pink. Her real bike is bigger and green. The second dream—I woke up (not really) because I heard noise downstairs. It was at night and my husband and I were in bed. I woke him up in the dream and told him, "I hear something downstairs." He said, "Don't move, I'll check it out!" I was concerned about my daughter, who was in the other bedroom. All of a sudden, we heard an alarm downstairs. He was very concerned and said, "Don't make a sound." I waited in the dark for him to check it out. I was very scared. I didn't hear him moving any longer. I couldn't figure it out, till I realized he had fallen back asleep. I yanked on his arm and tried to wake him. He just kept snoring away. I shook him and shook him and all he did was snore. Then I woke up to his real snoring in my ear.

More than anyone else in the world, Grace knew exactly how hard Richard pushed himself, and she couldn't help but wonder what would happen to the family if his strength and vigilance failed them. Married couples dream about each other all the time (we'll see another example later in the chapter with Dan and Sophia), and in Grace's case her dream creatively incorporated the actual sound of Richard's snoring into a hyperrealistic narrative about his inability to respond to a waking-world threat to the family. Here's another danger for her to worry about, another source of potential harm to her daughter, another problem to keep her on the psychological edge.

When Grace replied to the initial interview questions for this project I was immediately intrigued by what she described as her shifting political outlook. She characterized her political views as "liberal when I was younger, heading toward conservative as I age." In terms of party registration she says she's "Democratic but

I'm thinking of changing to Independent." Why, I wondered, are the Democrats losing a person like Grace? What's turning her into more of a conservative? A close study of her dreams suggests the reason is simple: the Democrats no longer represent the family values that form the core of her life. When she hears political debates about abortion, gay marriage, sex in movies and music, and so on, she finds herself increasingly alienated from the ideas and priorities of the Democratic leaders. She doesn't hear them saying anything that matters to the pressing reality of her hardworking, overstressed, financially strapped family situation. She's not necessarily a Republican, at least not yet. If nothing else, her liberal views on religion ("I'm really open to new ideas right now when it comes to my spirituality") directly clash with those of the fundamentalist Christians whose influence on the Republican Party has been so significant in recent years. But her days of being a true political liberal seem like ancient history to her. It's her growing anxiety regarding the need to protect her family that's driving the change in her political allegiance. She's moving away from the Democrats, toward . . . what? A disaffected "independence"? An eventual alignment with the Republicans? A temporary exile from the Democrats, which will end when a new leader articulates a genuinely liberal approach to the safeguarding of her family? She doesn't know herself. She says she's trying not to think about politics at all until the two parties have settled on their nominees. Then she'll watch the debates, size up each candidate, and make her choice. Grace is the American swing voter par excellence. The candidate who conveys to her the strongest feelings of sympathy, reassurance, and support for her family's economic difficulties will ultimately win her vote.

Dreaming and Sex

In many ways, America's political debate over family values can be reduced to a disagreement about the nature of human sexuality and its morally proper expression in society. Who can have sex with whom, where they can do it, when and why and how they can do it—these questions have sharply divided the Democratic and Republican parties for years, and will likely do so for many years to come. A typically conservative approach to sexuality regards it as something to be guarded and protected: sex is primarily a means of reproduction, and as such a legitimate good in human life, but its irrational power makes it dangerous to civil society and thus the proper subject of strict governmental control. A typically liberal approach understands sexuality not just as biological reproduction but also as a naturally fulfilling means of expressing love, intimacy, and joy; in this view, sexual freedom is a basic human right that should be sanctioned and protected by all governments.

In earlier research I found these political attitudes mirrored in people's dreams about sexuality.[1] Liberals reported a greater frequency of sexual dreams, with more detail and variety, than did conservatives. These data seemed like a good fit with their respective ideological positions, although it should be said that we'll never know for sure if conservatives dream less about sex or are less willing to talk about their sex dreams. That's a limiting factor in all research on people's sexual feelings and behavior. Either way, a similar pattern emerges in the latest sleep and dream poll, in which liberals reported more dreams of sexual experiences. The difference is not huge (47 percent versus 38 percent), but it's further psychological evidence of a conservative guardedness and liberal openness toward sexuality.

We can see the interplay of these dynamics in more detail in the dream journals of the focus group members. The two people who hold especially conservative views of family values, Grace and Dan, reported no sexual dreams at all. Again, this may be due to an understandable reluctance to write down the details of one's sexual dreams for analysis by a stranger. It's also due, perhaps, to the depth and power of their moral beliefs, which may enable them to control the potentially disruptive feelings of sexual desire that naturally arise in sleep. People like Grace and Dan may reach the point where they truly do not dream about anything manifestly sexual. On the other side, two of the most liberal people, Elizabeth and Kip, reported a number of sexual dreams involving various partners of both genders and bizarre fantasies of taboo-violating situations. Their political belief about the importance of sexual tolerance carries through in their dreaming, too, as they express their own sexual desires in a colorful variety of ways.

The conservative-liberal opposition takes a surprising twist, however, when we consider the sexual dreams of Richard and Paul. They reported a higher percentage of sexual dreams (8 percent of all his dreams for Richard, 14 percent for Paul) than anyone else in the group, including liberals like Elizabeth and Kip. Rather than conservative restraint, their dreaming selves liberally indulged in frequent and usually pleasurable sexual interactions with a variety of women, both known and unknown. Neither reported a dream of sex with another man—the taboo against homosexuality remained firm in their imaginations. In one dream Richard found himself confronted with an economically tempting challenge to violate several taboos:

> I dreamt that two lesbians that apparently lived together wanted to have a baby, but they didn't want to have to pay the high cost of artificial insemination. They asked if I would sleep with one of them because they researched my background and liked the idea that genetically I was artistic and musical, and they wanted their child to have my genes. One of the girls was very attractive, and she was the one that asked me to spend one night with her. I told her I couldn't because I was married, but that I found it to be an

exciting proposition and hard to say no, but I still couldn't. She then went to ask my wife, and told her she was willing to pay her $500 if she (my wife) would allow it. I was surprised because Grace said, yes we need the money!! Somehow the dream ended before anything happened.

At one level this is a glorious male fantasy of spreading one's seed, an ego-gratifying affirmation of genetic fitness. At another level it's a wry commentary on the family's financial situation and their eagerness to find new sources of income. The dream portrays a free market of human reproductive services that should horrify a family values conservative like Richard, yet this aspect doesn't seem to bother him. He's more surprised by his wife's willingness to release him from the sexual constraints of marriage and pursue this "exciting proposition" of serving as a professional stud. The Grace character in Richard's dream shares the waking Grace's concern with the family's financial situation, and Richard's sleeping imagination conjures up a truly creative wish fulfillment that allows him to have his cake and eat it, too.

Another factor complicating matters in the discussion of sexual dreams is the long history of Christian skepticism about the erotic temptations appearing within the sleeping imagination. Early Christian monks worried about the devil using such dreams to lure them away from their devotion to a chaste and celibate lifestyle. Theologians like Augustine, Aquinas, and Luther warned the faithful against the deceptive pleasures of sensually arousing dreams. Even today, many Christians in America associate dreams with demonic temptations and sinful lust, and in this belief they carry forward a time-honored church teaching: dreaming is a dangerous external force that interferes with the purity of one's moral self-control.

The problem for a dream researcher is that these Christians are right. Sexual arousal happens in dreaming all the time. There's an automatic process of increased blood flow to the genitals during REM sleep, producing erections in men and clitoral swelling in women on a regular basis throughout the sleep cycle. By its very nature, then, sleeping is a sexually stimulating experience. Not all dreams are directly related to sexual desire, but those that are explicitly sexual tend to develop in strange and morally discomforting directions. In some dreams people find themselves confronted with sexual feelings and desires they've never experienced in waking life. There's a frightening otherness to much of dream sexuality, a vulnerability to wild erotic energies whose pleasurable intensity can produce quite tangible effects on the dreamer's body upon awakening. If you belong to a religious tradition like Christianity (or Buddhism, for that matter) whose sacred principles include strict self-control over sexual desire, dreaming almost inevitably becomes a cause for concern and a target of moral regulation.

Shadows

Of all the focus group members, I've been most cautious in discussing Lola's life and dreams. I knew that keeping the journal would probably bring back upsetting emotions about the murder of her son, and I told her from the outset (as I told all the participants) that she was free to withdraw from the project at any time. Fortunately Lola is a resilient person with a great deal of psychological strength who enjoys thinking about her dreams and finds it comforting to talk about them. Her perspective is especially helpful at this point in the book, when we're discussing the political idealization of the American family. Lola has a different set of feelings about families. She's been forced to face the dark underside of family togetherness, to live out a Freudian nightmare of murderous sibling rivalry. Politicians may think that no amount of praise for "the family" is too much, but in so doing they neglect the shadow reality of contrary emotions that quietly dominate the lives of countless Americans. The honest psychological truth is that families are *not* always a source of comfort and well-being. The family environment itself has the potential to generate tensions and conflicts that can all too easily erupt in violence.

To her credit, Lola has not been shattered by that awful event, a severe psychological trauma by any definition. She relies for support on her husband, to whom she's been married for twenty-three years, and on her personal religious faith: "I haven't been to church in a few years but I pray and talk to God all the time. If it hadn't been for my faith, I think I would have died that day." She's a hardworking person who derives true satisfaction from her career as an administrator in assisted living facilities for the elderly and disabled. Her current job situation is a sore spot, however, and just like everyone else in the focus group she dreamed frequently and negatively about work. In terms of her feelings about her job, Lola is just as mentally healthy (or un-healthy) as anyone else. At a couple points during the year she had to give up the journal for long stretches because of extreme work stress, and I half expected she would soon drop out for that reason alone. But fortunately her employers hired a new person to take over some of her work, and immediately afterward she expe-rienced a rise in dream recall: "I think I was so stressed that I couldn't remember my dreams, and when he [the new employee] started the dreams started again."

Despite numerous disruptions, Lola managed to record more than one hundred dreams during the year. That makes her recall rate at least two dreams a week, and probably a good bit more than that. As she said in our first interview, Lola is an active dreamer who would be even more so if it weren't for the intense pressures of her job. She recorded her dreams in great detail (half of her reports were two hundred words or more), with one or two nightmares a month and a high percentage (42 percent) of dreams including a family member. Many of her dreams were bizarre, with strange shifts in the ages of people and animals (e.g., kittens changing suddenly into cats) and familiar buildings distorted in inexplicable ways. But several of the most common types of bizarreness were absent: she had no dreams of flying, lucidity, otherworldly realities, or magical powers. The majority of her dreams were mundane in representing recognizable, this-worldly settings and ordinary social interactions.

Recall that Lola considers herself a political conservative, and she voted twice for George W. Bush. She's pro-life, suspicious of big government, and favors more limits on immigration and control of the national borders: "We should take care of our own first before reaching out and allowing others to access our resources." These are classic conservative positions, and her sleep and dream patterns mostly agree with that political profile. I say mostly because her high recall rate and lengthy narratives suggest a more liberal perspective. She reported several sexual dreams, some with pleasurable experiences well outside the confines of marriage, reflecting a degree of openness about sexuality that's less typical of conservatives than of liberals. Much like Sophia, whose family-related dreams we'll discuss in a moment, Lola is a big dreamer from a mostly conservative point of view. Every day she fights to live out her vision of a good and meaningful life, despite her sad awareness of human frailty. She's politically conservative not because of any one issue or policy, but because of a deeper feeling of trust in the conservative emphasis on safety and security. At this point in life that's what she most wants from America's political leaders.

She voted twice for George W. Bush because she thought he could provide security for the country. But recently Lola has found herself questioning his ability to deal effectively with America's problems. After the death of her youngest son, Lola spent many years taking care of a nephew whose family situation had become dangerous for his welfare. During the journal-keeping year this nephew turned twenty-one, enlisted in the army, and was promptly sent to Iraq. Naturally, Lola felt very anxious about the dangers he would be facing. She said this situation was the background to the following dream, which occurred during the period when President Bush's plan for a new "surge" of troops was just starting to be publicly discussed:

A guy I work with, (Jim), and his wife, (Susan), and I are trying to cross a bridge. We are on a flat cart with no sides, sort of like a carpet ride. The three of us are zooming very fast on a path. We go up a big hill of water, down and up and over. We come to a bridge that is being built. There are men everywhere with weapons. We try to reason with them to let us cross. They take Susan away. Jim and I are locked up in an open cage overlooking the construction of the bridge. The men are ogling Susan. Jim is getting crazy. I tell him to keep his cool, that is the only way we are going to escape. I look out and see a woman in the distance. She is winking at me and motions for me to look down. I see a way to escape... We find Susan and the woman in the distance winks at us to go. We are back on the cart again on a wild ride. Up and over we go... We see a big crowd ahead. It is a stadium, and President Bush is there speaking. We glide right up to him and tell him he must pull the troops out of Iraq, because we have our own war going on right here. We tell him about the men at the bridges that we just escaped. He tells us not to worry; he will take care of it.

Another bridge nightmare—another example showing how cultural metaphors weave their way into personal dreams.[2] In Lola's case the bridge is an image of controlled movement, physical coercion, and unexpected violence; the people who control the bridge are controlling her life. She and her friends manage to escape (thanks to the help of the enigmatic winking woman), but Lola knows the bad guys are still there, back at the bridge. That's when the magic cart suddenly brings them someplace new, to what appears to be a large political rally for President Bush. Lola would usually be a member of that crowd, but in this dream she's approaching the president from a very different direction. Without any hesitation she and her friends float up to him and deliver a clear, plainspoken message that would please even the most fervent antiwar Democrat. The president tries to reassure her, but Lola says the dream ends on an ambiguous note, with her uncertainty as to whether or not he'll heed her request.

Here, then, is a stirring of significant political discontent that's pushing a traditionally conservative person away from the president and his Republican supporters. Lola isn't sure any more that fighting a war in Iraq is the best way to keep America safe, and she's terrified at the thought of losing another close relative for such a doubtful cause. *We have our own war going on right here*—that's the cry of a conservative backlash against the president's risky plans for nation building in the Middle East. Lola and many conservatives like her are tired of claims about the importance of solving Iraq's problems when they see so many unsolved problems here in America. She hasn't yet acted on these feelings in terms of her voting behavior (she feels a deep distrust toward Hillary Clinton), but a dream like this suggests she's becoming increasingly open to candidates from either party who emphasize the urgency of bringing U.S. soldiers home quickly and safely. For Lola, the war has truly become a matter of family values.

New Birth

When Dan left for his third tour in Iraq, Sophia confronted the very real possibility that her unborn child's father would never return. In some ways, however, being pregnant gave Sophia's life a focus during those dark and lonely times that she would not have otherwise had. Her toddler daughter, Mandy, took an avid interest in Sophia's growing tummy, and the familiar rhythms of her body's changes from month to month became an unexpected source of comfort. Looking at her dreams, it's difficult to sort out the influences of pregnancy from the other sources of stress and concern in her life, but a few details stand out. Like Dan, she had a dream the night before they found out for sure she was pregnant; her report was a very brief one by her standards:

> Tried hard to remember, something to do with babies and being lost and found.

The irony was that she and Dan had just discussed whether or not they wanted to have more children, and they had decided no, they couldn't. The prospect of another baby in their lives was truly lost, then found again. When the pregnancy tests came back positive, a floodgate of dreaming opened up—three or four dreams a night for almost two weeks. This intense upsurge of dreaming activity released all the emotional energy that was stirred up by this surprising new development in her life. She said the dreams helped her sort through the complex implications of being pregnant again—the impact on her marriage, her care of Mandy, her body, her school plans, family finances, the need for a new house, and so on. One night during this dreaming blitz she and Dan both dreamed of her being kidnapped. In his version, she was taken captive by some of her friends, who wanted to use her for nefarious sexual purposes; he wasn't worried, though, because he knew where Sophia was. He felt in control of the situation. In her version, she was separated from Dan at a civic center and found herself being held hostage by strangely behaving friends she had known earlier in her life. She tried to call Dan several times, and when she finally reached him he matter-of-factly told her to get in the car and drive home. She was trying to get out of danger, but she wasn't sure she could do it alone. Their dreaming imaginations were working in tandem to prepare for the dangers and difficulties to come.

Consistent with other studies of pregnant women's dreams, Sophia reported a variety of animal dreams during the journal-keeping year (about one in six of her dreams had an animal character). She reported a fairly high number of nightmares (thirty-six by my count), but these seemed to be related more to her worries about Dan than about the pregnancy itself—she reported big spikes in bad dreams the month before his deployment and the month after he arrived in Iraq. Almost half her dreams involved someone in her family, true to her major waking-life preoccupations at the time. However, a majority of Sophia's dreams were quite bizarre in terms of fantastic settings and unrealistic behavior, evidence, I think, of a highly active imagination reaching beyond the confines of present reality to envision different possibilities for the future. The sense of limitless potential stimulated by these dreams provided Sophia with a psychological counterbalance to the constraining pressures of her waking-world situation.

The months passed. Dan's unit saw frequent combat in some rough parts of Iraq, but he made it safely through each mission. Sophia got bigger and rounder, and toward the end she dreamed twice the child would be a boy (they hadn't tested for the baby's gender). Her obstetrician said everything was going well, the delivery date was just a few days away... and finally the army granted Dan's request to return home in time for the birth. Their relief when he arrived can easily be imagined. Dan was now home for good, only months away from the end of his military service, a time when he could retire with benefits, live at home with his family, and think about starting a new career. Sophia no longer had to fear the prospect of becoming a war widow; her young children would have both parents to care for them, and she would have her husband back.

Fate would not let them off so easily, however. Her delivery date came, and it went. Days passed, and while she and her obstetrician were discussing when to induce labor, Dan received cruel news from Iraq—his unit had been caught in an ambush, and one of his closest team members was killed. Sophia knew the friend's wife and family well, and the next several days were consumed with helping them emotionally cope, preparing for the return of the body, and planning the memorial service. Sophia said these were some of the hardest days she and Dan had ever gone through with their friends in the military community.

The day after the memorial, Sophia went into labor. A few hours later she delivered a healthy baby boy.

Conclusion

Why do people believe what they believe about politics? That's the question behind everything discussed in this book. Where do the passions and principles come from that inspire Americans of so many different varieties to advocate certain political causes and oppose others? In my view it's not because of people's genes, or brains, or family upbringings, although each of those factors seems to play a role.[1] It's certainly not because people rationally analyze the pros and cons of all the various policy positions. Conscious reasoning usually has little say in the matter. It's not even because the 24/7 news media are deviously manipulating people's thoughts and emotions. The psychological roots of people's political beliefs lie deeper than that. As I've tried to show, they reach all the way down into the dream world of each individual's ultimate ideals, the core values expressing his or her fundamental vision of what life is and can become. Dreams don't simply mirror people's political beliefs; they provide the raw psychological material for those beliefs. In dreaming we find an emotionally honest portrayal of each individual's greatest hopes, concerns, desires, and aspirations, all of which feed directly into the belief systems that guide his or her waking life. This is why I believe a political ideology is best seen as a metaphorical *and* literal dream of collective coexistence. In politics we seek to actualize within social reality the ideals we believe are most important in life. The psychological appeal of a political ideology can thus be measured by how well its dreams harmonize with the dreams of other members of society. The most successful politicians will be those who cultivate the deepest intuitive understanding of the dream experiences of the community as a whole.

Politicians in the United States today face a country whose people seem to be losing faith in the promise of the American Dream.[2] Most people continue to share a basic belief in what that dream means—the freedom to create one's own life, the opportunity to succeed through initiative and hard work, the hope that tomorrow will be better than today. But they're increasingly uncertain about the dream's future survival, and they worry their children will grow up to face a world of worsening prospects. Politicians who fail to acknowledge this gathering gloom and who try instead to peddle a sunny optimism about America's future will, I suspect, have a very difficult time gaining much popular support. And yet, politicians who focus only on anxieties and problems and who fail to reignite a deep, energizing sense of faith in the American Dream will find it much harder to rally the country toward creative solutions to the challenges that lie ahead. It appears an impossible combination, but that's what the times are calling for. We need realistic dreamers, practical visionaries. We need leaders whose breadth of command is rooted in the depths of the creative imagination.

I doubt the information presented in this book will change your mind about your party registration, voting preferences, approval or disapproval of President Bush, or anything like that. Perhaps some readers will find themselves tending in a more liberal direction once they discover for themselves the boundary-crossing

creativity of dreaming. Others might become more conserva-
tively inclined after witnessing in dreams further evidence of the
unruly animal impulses that dwell within each of us and con-
stantly threaten social order. Ultimately, you will have to be the
judge of your own realizations. I believe (along with most other
present-day researchers and therapists) that only the dreamer can
ever know for sure what his or her dreams mean. Only *you* have
direct experiential access to the feelings, images, and atmospheric
sensations of your dreams. Only you know the memory associations and waking-life references that can fully make sense of all
their details. Other people may give you helpful suggestions and
offer possible interpretations, but in the end it's always your personal evaluation that's decisive.

Whatever you discover in your future oneiric adventures, I
hope you've found in the preceding pages a new way of thinking
about your political views and those of other Americans. The
method I've followed is based on a simple idea: *exploring the nocturnal side of human existence leads to new insight into people's waking
beliefs and behaviors.* Following this kind of integrative approach
leads to a richer and more complete portrait of the political psychology of contemporary America. Taking people's sleeping and
dreaming experiences into account provides a source of depth
psychological information that's difficult to gain from surveys of
waking attitudes alone. Looking at politics through this prism
enables us to see not just *what* people believe but *why* they believe
it—why it makes deep intuitive sense for them to support certain
political causes and not others, why they feel attracted to some
candidates and not others, why they fear particular threats and
dangers, why they hope for certain visions of future prosperity.
If you know what people are dreaming, you'll know what they
most deeply value and what they're most likely to seek in a political leader.

Comparisons

The data presented in this book for the most part agree with the findings of my earlier studies. Political conservatives in America tend to sleep well, with a diminished range of dreaming, while American liberals are more likely to sleep poorly, with an expanded range of dreaming. The differences are not absolute, but the trends seem consistent with their respective political ideals.

These findings correspond fairly well with other research on political psychology. For example, John T. Jost and his colleagues argued in an influential 2003 article that "the core ideology of conservatism stresses resistance to change and justification of inequality and is motivated by needs that vary situationally and dispositionally to manage uncertainty and threat."[3] Reviewing the results of eighty-eight studies involving more than twenty thousand people, Jost et al. found that political conservatism was psychologically correlated with high degrees of death anxiety and dogmatism and low degrees of openness to experience, tolerance of uncertainty, and integrative complexity. Without corresponding data on political liberals it's hard to know exactly what to make of these findings, but they seem consistent in many ways with the patterns identified in my dream research, and thus supportive of a classic social scientific view of conservatives going back to Adorno and his 1950 study of "the authoritarian personality." Conservatives seem to have thicker psychological boundaries than do liberals, with less interest in anything that deviates from their traditional ways of living and more concern about possible threats to those traditions.[4]

My hesitation to fully endorse this line of research stems from (1) its pathologizing approach to conservative beliefs and ideals; and (2) its premise that there's a clear, stable distinction between a conservative and a liberal personality. I believe it's better to start political psychology research with the recognition that no one is purely conservative or liberal. Everybody's personality includes aspects of both tendencies. If you've got a bank account, you're at least a little conservative; you want to guard and protect your money. If you like watching television or listening to radio and having different channels to choose from, you're at least somewhat liberal; you value cultural diversity and freedom of expression. I'm not the first to make this argument, but my research adds further evidence to bolster the point: Americans cannot be neatly divided into two separate ideological categories. The sleep and dream patterns of the dreamers' focus group revealed an intricate interweaving of conservative and liberal feelings in each of the ten people. This suggests that Americans are far more psychologically complex and multifaceted than is usually recognized. We share more in common than we know; our differences are matters of degree, not kind. Even though the Republican and Democratic parties benefit from exaggerating their dissimilarities (the demonization of others remains a powerful tool of mass persuasion), the reality is that most people incorporate both conservative and liberal values in their daily behaviors. When we speak of someone being a conservative or liberal person, then, we're talking about which set of values they emphasize the most, not about a fixed, either-or characteristic of human nature.

Looking in another comparative direction, the approach I've used here has a strong affinity with that of George Lakoff, a cognitive linguist at the University of California, Berkeley. Lakoff's work on conceptual metaphors has deeply influenced my interpretive method, particularly his idea that the same metaphor-generating capacities the mind uses while awake are also active in dreaming.[5] In 1996 Lakoff wrote *Moral Politics,* a book investigating the metaphorical dimensions of political rhetoric. He found the Republican Party made frequent use of "Strict Father" metaphors to describe their conservative approach to government, while the Democrats favored metaphors of the "Nurturing Parent" to express their liberal values.[6] This quasi-psychoanalytic way of analyzing American political beliefs has merit, although it's difficult to apply in a rigorous and convincing way to the material we've been discussing in this book. A few dreams could probably be found that exemplify one or the other perspective, but I'm always wary of starting with a specific theoretical model and then looking for instances to confirm it. I prefer looking at the dreams themselves and trying to identify their basic patterns of form and content, patterns that can be easily recognized and agreed upon by multiple observers. We can make a lot of progress, and avoid many unnecessary arguments, by following that approach.

I've made no claims regarding the psychotherapeutic implications of my findings, but I do see an immediate connection to the work of Andrew Samuels, a Jungian analyst in Britain. In his 1993 book *The Political Psyche* he looked at the connections between people's psychological development and their practical engagement in political activism. Based on clinical and cultural evidence, Samuels argued that psychological growth naturally prompts political growth. Adaptive changes in the power dynamics of inner life have the potential to stimulate comparable transformations in the power dynamics of outer life. However, Samuels found that psychotherapists often fail to recognize this process when their clients bring overtly political material into the clinical setting. I share Samuels's desire to expand our conception of "the political," and my research provides support for his general idea that politics "refers to a crucial interplay between these two dimensions, between the private and public dimensions of power."[7] Like Samuels, I encourage psychotherapists to take their clients' political beliefs more seriously as the healthy expressions of a growing psyche.

Samuels, like Lakoff, is an avowed political liberal, and Jost et al. leave little doubt as to their greater sympathy for liberal qualities. The leftward-leaning tendencies of most social scientists give us good reason to question the motivations of researchers who argue that conservatives are somehow less mentally healthy or psychologically mature than liberals. Personal bias plays a role in political psychology just as it does in every academic field, and the best we researchers can do is try to be honest with ourselves and continually test our ideas against new sources of evidence. Speaking for myself, I would certainly locate myself on the leftward side of the political spectrum, but I feel a kinship with many different perspectives (I was raised in a Republican family, and became Libertarian in my teens; I mostly vote Democratic now, with Green Party leanings). I've known enough smart conservatives and dumb liberals in my life to dispel any illusion that my political perspective represents the apex of psychological development.

This book has pointed out several places where the sleep and dream findings illuminate the relative strengths of both liberals and conservatives. Having briefly mentioned a few liberal social scientists, let me also mention a conservative theologian whose analysis of American politics resonates with the sleep and dream findings. Reinhold Niebuhr (1892–1971) was a Protestant pastor and professor of Christian ethics whose teachings on the proper use of power in society have influenced America's conservative Christians for the last several decades. Niebuhr pushed back against the truth-claims of the social sciences, arguing that their rationalist theories inevitably fail to do justice to the subtle organic complexities of individual life and collective behavior. He rejected the assumption that scientific reason represents the standard by which all human knowing should be measured, and he called for greater awareness of religion's central role in advancing the welfare of society:

[T]here must always be a religious element in the hope of a just society. Without the ultrarational hopes and passions of religion no society will ever have the courage to conquer despair and attempt the impossible; for the vision of a just society is an impossible one, which can be approximated only by those who do not regard it as impossible... To the sensitive spirit, society must always remain something of the jungle, which indeed it is, something of the world of nature, which might be brought a little nearer the kingdom of God, if only the sensitive spirit could learn, how to use the forces of nature to defeat nature, how to use force in order to establish justice. Knowing the peril of corruption in this strategy, the religious spirit recoils. If that fear can be overcome, religious ideals may yet achieve social and political significance.[8]

This passage beautifully expresses the religious and political sentiments of conservatives like Richard, Grace, Paul, Lola, Dan, and Sophia. They all have humble expectations about what's possible in this life, and a keen awareness of the frailty and fallibility of human nature. Nevertheless, they remain actively and energetically engaged with the world, trying to live up to high standards of competence, control, and personal responsibility, striving to put into practice the deeper truths they trust more than they reasonably should. The virtue of courage looms large in their vision of life, the courage to believe that one's actions are divinely meaningful despite the inevitability of conflict, suffering, failure, and death. For each of the group members, conservatives and liberals, I've tried to identify where they display this virtue in their waking and dreaming lives. Just as Niebuhr described it, I've found all of them struggling to overcome their fears and use whatever powers they possess to put their ideals into practice.

To formulate a dream and envision a better future requires the imaginative openness of a liberal; to hold onto that dream against the relentless, dispiriting blows of fortune requires the strength and courage of a conservative.

The Union

Is it too fantastic to suggest that Americans might benefit from trying to incorporate the best elements of each political perspective? Sleeping well like the conservatives and creatively dreaming like the liberals? Perhaps this kind of cognitive flexibility can only develop if it's nurtured early in life, before one's belief system has become too fixed and hardened. But I would argue, following an insight of Jung's, that people always maintain a capacity for *political individuation*—a lifelong process by which they develop and actualize the full range of their innate psychological powers, including the classic political virtues of conservatism and liberalism. What precise form that political individuation might take for each person, I can't say. But I do know from many years of studying dreams that when the conscious mind makes a deliberate effort to strengthen and expand its awareness in a new direction, the unconscious mind responds with a spontaneous surge of imagery, insight, and emotional energy. The back-and-forth dynamic of conscious intention and unconscious creativity leads to new psychological growth, what Jung called the *coniunctio oppositorum,* or "union of opposites." I dream of a time when Americans develop the psychological capacity to unite the opposites of our political culture—enacting progressive social change without losing traditional wisdom, safeguarding time-honored values while remaining open to new ways of living.

Appendix 1

Dreams of Politics and Politicians

This appendix presents a number of politically related dreams gathered from my research and other sources. In some cases I've been able to ask the individuals follow-up questions about the details and waking-life circumstances of their dreams. In other cases such information comes from secondary sources, or is not available. The difficulty in verifying the authenticity of anecdotal reports like these makes it unwise to put too much weight on them as evidence in arguing for a dreaming-politics connection. That's why I focused the main body of the book on analyzing the systematically gathered data from the sleep and dream poll and the long-term dream journals. Now that we've used that data to establish a good empirical foundation, we can feel more confident in hazarding interpretations of a set of politically related dream reports that highlight many of the themes discussed earlier in the book.

Terrorism School

In my dream, I am taking my "last college course" which I must take to graduate. In response to September 11th, it is a "Terrorism" course, in which we as the students are treated like hostages of terrorists, in order to understand what that feels like. This class is very real, and we are blindfolded and tied to each other and forced to walk around an empty, cold warehouse, falling down stairs and knocking into walls. I am so frightened and I keep trying to speak to the other students and convince them that this is an outrageous class and a violation of our rights, but whenever I speak up, I am hit across the face. I'm scared that these folks really are terrorists and have fooled the school administration and are really going to torture and kill us. When they take our blindfolds off, we are lined up and given guns. We have to shoot the gun at a small glass of blood between our feet. The idea is that we must learn to shoot straight, or we will shoot ourselves in the foot, and if we hit the glass correctly, the blood will splash up into our face, giving us the direct feeling of shooting someone at point-blank range and having the blood splash onto us. I am scared out of mind at this point, and I watch as some students hit their target, and others shoot themselves in the foot. They are not given any medical attention. I decide in my mind that I will shake my hand so severely that they will have to let me go without shooting...I also think about aiming the gun at the teachers of the class and rescuing as many of us as I can. (Thus making me a terrorist?)

Martha told me she had this dream the night of September 11, 2006. She's a thirty-four-year-old artist and teacher from California who was an eyewitness to the 9/11 attack in New York (another dream of hers is discussed below). She's strongly opposed to President Bush and his Iraq war policy, and her dark feelings about the country emerge quite vividly in the grotesque imagery of the dream. Ever since 9/11 liberals have feared an excessively aggressive and xenophobic reaction from the United States toward anyone suspected of being a terrorist, and many of those fears have indeed come true. Martha's feelings of fear, paralysis, confusion, and frustration are widely shared among the antiwar liberals, who see America becoming so obsessed with terrorism that it risks becoming a terrorist state itself. The bloody horrors of war are amplified by the obscene brutality of popular culture (Martha had just watched the David Cronenberg film *A History of Violence*). Martha's dream reminds me of the reports gathered by Charlotte Beradt in her 1966 book *The Third Reich of Dreams,* in which she described the fearful dreams of social control and political pressure experienced by Germans from 1933 to 1939, during the rise of National Socialism. I don't want to push the analogy too far, but there's no question the post-9/11 trend in the United States has been toward greater constraints on personal freedom, more hostility toward our perceived enemies, and more governmental intrusion in people's lives. Martha's dream articulates the ultimate fear of American liberals—that once civil liberties begin to erode, it gets harder and harder to stop the slide toward governmental tyranny and de facto dictatorship.

The Fate of Joe Lieberman

He [Lieberman] was feeling loose now, so much so that he began telling aides about a dream he'd had the other night in which long-dead Democratic Connecticut governor John Dempsey had walked across a stage and waved at him. Lieberman was puzzled by the dream. It was hard not to wonder what his unconscious was telling him: Was this the Democratic organization from the past wishing the senator well or waving goodbye?

—Meryl Gordon, "Joe Lieberman's War: The Hawkish Senator Finds Himself in an Epic Battle—With His Own Party," *New York Magazine,* August 7, 2006.

On August 8, Lieberman, the incumbent Democratic senator from Connecticut, lost the Democratic primary to newcomer Ned Lamont, whose antiwar campaign stirred up sufficient liberal opposition to reject Lieberman and his unwavering support for President Bush's campaign in Iraq. His defeat seemed to mark the end of his career, a dramatic and precipitous fall given that just six years earlier he was the Democratic vice presidential candidate alongside Al Gore. Lieberman did not accept defeat, however. Instead he ran as an independent in the November 2006 general election and handily beat Lamont, retaining his senate seat for a fourth term. From our vantage today, his puzzling dream visitation from the late governor (Dempsey died in 1989) might qualify as a kind of prophetic anticipation of the political near-death experience he was about to endure. (Lieberman, an observant Jew, would likely know of his religious tradition's long belief in the prophetic power of dreaming, especially in times of mortal danger.) Lieberman did indeed come within hailing distance of his political demise. A classic theme in visitation dreams is a welcoming gesture from the dead, which is often interpreted as a sign that the dreamer will soon depart this world and journey to the next. After he lost the primary, Lieberman could have accepted the Democratic voters' verdict, followed the path taken by Dempsey (a loyal member of the state's Democratic Party who retired in 1971), and left the political scene. Instead he fought against the Democrats, and won. He survived the threat to his political life, but perhaps at the cost of losing connection with his ideological ancestors.

The All-Powerful

I had a dream that Dick Cheney had found a way to "steal time" from the future, to prolong the present. Bastard.

Neil, a thirty-two-year-old Democrat, was suffering a terrible head cold when he had this nightmare in early 2006. The dream did not improve his spirits.

It's All My Fault

In the dream I am sitting on my sofa in the apartment I was living in four years ago, watching the election night news on TV with my fiancé. That part is more like remembering the night of the last election. The news analyst announces the results of each state's votes and who they'll support. They are pretty much even, until suddenly the announcer says that all the states have changed their votes for Bush, and Bush will be the president again. The announcer looks right at me and adds, "because he (Bush) doesn't like YOU, NINA!" My stomach sinks and I realize that it's all my fault. I wake up feeling affronted and guilty and out of breath.

Nina was a twenty-seven-year-old graduate student in North Carolina, very liberal in her political views and worried about the upcoming 2004 presidential election. She had this dream several times in the weeks leading up to the November vote, another extremely close contest involving President Bush and the Democratic nominee, John Kerry. Nina said, "The dream is haunting because it's a mixture of remembering events and feelings from the last presidential election and anxiety that it will happen again." The exaggerated sense of guilt she feels reflects a broader sentiment felt among a large number of Americans (Kerry received 59 million votes, 48 percent of the total ballots cast, in a losing cause). Despite the best efforts of Democrats, America elected Bush to a second term as president. Liberals couldn't help feeling personally responsible for letting the country decline so far so fast.

165

President Bush Saves the Dog

I was at the White House, and for some reason there were a bunch of rottweiler dogs being put to sleep for being too dangerous. The lady that was administering the shot was just about to inject the last dog when President Bush came downstairs to take his dog out. I asked if I could talk to him, and he said sure. I walked with him outside and told him how upset I was about the dogs being put to sleep. We were alone on the lawn, and I asked him why there was no security outside, and he just shrugged his shoulders and smiled. He told me I could have the last dog if I wanted it. We went back inside and the president grabbed the shot out of the lady's hand, and there was a brief struggle. The dog came running over to me and was wagging its tail, and I was so excited to be taking it home. I remember looking at the dog and seeing the colors of his fur (black with brown spots), and also when walking with the president, I saw the color of his jacket (green).

Susan was a twenty-three-year-old Republican woman from Pennsylvania who worked for Bush during the 2004 campaign. She said the dream accurately reflected her feelings about the "good things" the president has done in office, with Bush appearing as a "down-to-earth guy" whom she can trust to soothe her worries. He makes this special gesture of compassion for a loyal supporter, showing Susan the exact personal qualities that have attracted her to Bush in waking life. However, she didn't know what to make of the strange process of dog slaughter, nor of the president's uncharacteristic lack of concern about security. Even in the dream of a loyal Republican, the Bush White House appears haunted by mysteries and hidden motives.

Helping the Cause

I am teaching classes to new airmen on nuclear, biological, and chemical warfare. I was in civilian clothes and we were in a classroom.

James was a thirty-six-year-old graduate student and former air force weapons specialist when the Iraq war started in 2003, and in the months leading up to the invasion he had several dreams like this. James was a strong supporter of President Bush's approach to Iraq, and while he served in the air force his training focused on weapons of mass destruction, "so I think the dreams have to do with wanting to help in an area that I know." Like Richard's dream of serving the country as an Iraqi translator but more plausibly related to actual life, James repeatedly envisioned the role he could play for America during a time of war. He's another soldier preparing himself in recurrent dreams to join the battle.

Personal Symbol

I am waiting at a crosswalk, trying to get across the street. The warning light is flashing alternately green and red in rapid succession: WALK, DON'T WALK, WALK, DON'T WALK, WALK, etc. At the same time, cars with anonymous drivers are whizzing by. I am active in trying to get across the street, trying to time my sprint between the cars. One car comes along that is occupied by several people whom I recognize as citizens of Iraq, from all walks of life. Walking, I cross the street comfortably and safely after they pass.

What I call "personal symbols" are dream references to political figures or events that metaphorically express some kind of emotionally significant issue in the dreamer's personal life. Such dreams correspond to Frederick Perls's notion that every feature of a dream represents a part of the dreamer's own psyche. They also relate to Jung's view that some dreams can be interpreted at a "subjective level" by which all the images reflect internal psychological dynamics. Several of the political dreams I've gathered include personal symbols in this sense, such as this one from Kerri, a thirty-nine-year-old college counselor. She dreamed it on March 21, 2003, two days after the U.S. invasion of Iraq began. Regarding the Iraq conflict, Kerri said she was not strongly opposed or in favor—"I am for peace but support war when necessary." She felt this dream had nothing to do with Iraq but rather was "purely personal" and related directly to a problematic relationship in her current life—"in my dream (and in reality) it's clear that I'm going to walk, the question is when." The presence of the Iraqi people driving quickly past her does not refer to anything in particular about the war in Iraq, but rather serves to emphasize this personal life theme of movement, change, and translocation—she's going to take decisive action to end a problematic situation.

The Earth Is Cracking

We were in an area of land—this bad guy (dictatorlike— no clear features but dark hair, medium height and build) had a key to break up one part of the land. Someone else had another key, which was a disc (small like a coin, silver-gray colored—sometimes plastic, looking other times more metallic in appearance). The bad guy got a hold of that key, too. I think he used the keys. We were running (who was not clear—may not have been me—there was a female with brown straight hair). The land started to crack beneath the group, and oceans of water lay underneath. I awoke feeling terrified or an adrenaline rush—like fight-

or-flight reaction. At the same time it felt like I was watching a *Star Trek* adventure or like I was in outer space or on another planet.

Some dreams relate to political feelings even if they have no explicitly political images. Sandra, a forty-one-year-old woman, dreamed this on March 20, 2003, right after the Iraq invasion began. She said the dream "nagged at me throughout the day," and she knew it related directly to the war, even though she had not been paying much attention to the media coverage of the conflict. "I'm sure the earth cracking is metaphoric of how I feel about this whole world situation and that the ocean lies underneath reminds me of just how powerful the ocean can be (reminds me of cycle of birth, death, and rebirth)." The bad guy is certainly reminiscent of Iraqi leader Saddam Hussein, although the fact that the dream character remains a more generalized antagonist points to a deeper level of emotional distress—Sandra is not simply afraid of Saddam Hussein, she is afraid of how the war in Iraq is setting loose destructive powers that threaten the very foundations of the world. The ocean underneath hints at a dimension of spiritual hope amid the fear and panic, although the science fiction framing at the end may reflect a wish that none of this is really happening.

9/11 Vision

I'm walking through a forest that has been chopped down. It is a sea of stumps. Every single tree has been cut. I stand in the middle, sobbing. Who could do this? I walk up to one of the stumps and see the huge, beautiful spiral inside. I get lost in its magnificence. These trees are so old. I can see all of history in these trees, and I'm struck with the beauty and power of seeing this part of the tree. It's a part that I don't get to see. This spiral is taking me so deeply down into myself, to a place so powerful that it overwhelms me.

Martha was twenty-nine years old and visiting a friend in New York City on September 11, 2001. Her friend worked at the World Trade Center, and when Martha heard news of the attack she rode her bike to the waterfront, where she stood in shock and watched both towers collapse. After several frantic hours she discovered her friend had survived. That night Martha had this dream. She said she woke up the next morning with the oneiric feeling of mysterious power carrying over into her waking awareness. She felt "so much calmer and clear-headed," and she said the beautiful image of the spiral helped her get through the agonies of the next day. Because she was a direct witness of the destruction of the WTC towers, Martha's dream gives an especially clear illustration of how the dreaming imagination transforms waking events into metaphorical expressions. The dream is clearly related to the horrifying sights of that day, but it doesn't present those sights in a direct and literal fashion. Rather than showing the WTC towers collapsing, Martha's night vision portrays a forest whose trees have been cruelly and inexplicably chopped down. The symbolic connection between the towers and the trees is plainly evident, and yet what I think is most interesting is the way Martha's dream goes *beyond* the obvious connections to explore important dimensions of the disaster that may not, in all the fear and frenzy of that day, have been fully appreciated by her conscious awareness. In the dream her attention is drawn not to the destruction of two very tall buildings, but to the wanton murder of a whole community of living beings. All her sadness and horror and confusion are focused on this desolate image of the razed forest; all the terrible emotions of the previous day find expression at this moment.

Then something new happens, something so powerful that it crosses over from the dream world into Martha's waking awareness. As she is walking through the "sea of stumps" (an evocative phrase itself), she goes over to one of the stumps and sees "the huge beautiful spiral inside." Martha realizes she's seeing something usually hidden from view, and she finds herself carried away with the ever-deepening movement of the spiral, all the way to a place of ancient power and overwhelming beauty. When she woke up, those positive, revitalizing feelings were still very much with her. To be sure, Martha still felt scared and confused about what was going on in the waking world, but her dream had succeeded in bringing new energies into her conscious awareness. If the trees had not been cut down, she never would have seen the beautiful spiral; if the terrorist attack had not occurred, she never would have needed to reach so far into her own psychospiritual depths. Out of tragedy comes hope; out of destruction, new life.

Election Night 2000

I kept seeing those stupid Electoral College maps on TV turning red, then blue, then red again. It was a very fitful night's sleep.

Cloris, a thirty-two-year-old woman from California, reported this on November 2, 2000, the night of the 2000 presidential election. That night produced what may have been the most collectively sleep-deprived moment of American history. Virtually every person working in politics, government, and the news media, along with tens of millions of partisan supporters and fascinated onlookers, stayed awake that whole night in a state of anxious uncertainty. Given what we know from medical science about the harmful consequences of sleep deprivation (diminished cognitive skills, weakened emotional self-control, loss

171

of physical coordination and immunological health), that next day, November 3, marked a brief but extreme period of national vulnerability, with the entirety of the country's political leadership and a large portion of the general population functioning at unusually low levels of mental and physical well-being. If there was ever a time when an enemy assault would have been most likely to succeed, when our government would be least capable of responding effectively, it was the hours and days following the 2000 election.

Paradoxically, what followed that night was not an external attack, but rather an internal crisis of identity. The defining image of that crisis was the electoral-map nightmare of a country split almost exactly in half between red states and blue states, conservatives and liberals, heartland Republicans and coastal Democrats. In the brightly colored graphics that filled everyone's television screens on that preposterous night, the lines between the two sides were sharply drawn. Their ideological positions were fixed, their geographical identities clear, their contempt for each other intense and entirely mutual. The 2000 election did not create this partisan division, but the bizarre circumstances surrounding the election had the effect of burning the red state versus blue state conflict more deeply into people's minds than ever before.

Golfing with Bill

I'm playing golf with Bill Clinton. I've heard people say he cheats, and I understand what they mean, because he frequently improves the lie of his ball. But he encourages the people he's playing with to do the same. He says, "It's just a game, and just for fun!"

This dreamer, a thirty-six-year-old man, voted enthusiastically for Clinton in 1992. But in the summer of 1996, when he told me this dream, he wasn't sure if he would vote for Clinton in the upcoming election. He saw the golf imagery of his dream as an amusingly apt expression of his concern that President Clinton is a "cheater" who frequently "improves his lies" and then tries to smooth-talk other people into letting him get away with it.

Perot Mania

For some reason I was going to work at a state mental hospital which was being closed down. People were carrying files out, wheeling patients away. It was a big, dingy building. I and some others were waiting for the new boss to come. Much to our surprise, Ross Perot arrived. He stated that he would be running the hospital and we would work for him. He was dressed casually in a tacky purple and white outfit. He looked ridiculous. The rest of the staff gathered, and instead of taking the elevator we all walked up the stairs to prove our dedication and endurance. The climb was longer than expected and we were all complaining and some people were sick. Ross didn't know how much farther we had to go, anymore than we did...Although there were nurses there, none would help him but me. Ross didn't know what to do.

When I first began studying politically related dreams in 1992, the candidate who appeared most often in the reports I gathered was Ross Perot, a charismatic businessman who founded the Reform Party and ran for president against the Republican incumbent, George H. W. Bush, and the Democratic challenger, Bill Clinton. For a time Perot was leading both Bush and Clinton in national polls. The media spotlight on the quirky, irascible Texan became intense as Americans pondered the idea of him actually becoming president. The frequency of people dreaming about Perot matched his seeming omnipresence in the national media. This dream came from Jean, a thirty-two-year-old woman who worked in a department store and whose political views tended to be center-left. She agreed with Perot on the severity of the country's financial problems, but she felt he was an entirely inappropriate person to occupy the White House. She told me she felt the dream was a commentary on the "lunacy" of the country and the "double lunacy" of thinking "a crazy man could be the leader of a mental hospital."

Clinton for a Change

I am on the top of a high-rise building, looking across the way into an apartment's picture window...I am with someone I feel comfortable with, although this person's identity is unknown to me. Through the apartment window I see a half dozen or more owls looking out...I then look down to my right and see Bill Clinton seated beside me. My feeling is one of slight surprise and friendliness toward him. I immediately say, "Oh, hi, Clinton...I'm sorry but I can't recall your first name...You know, with the continual emphasis on the name Clinton by the media..." He responds that his name is Bill, and we exchange conversational niceties of "Glad to meet you's," while continuing to observe the owls.

In the fall of 1992 when she had this dream, Patty was a young woman working at an accounting firm in a big city. Although her job paid well, she wasn't happy with it and wanted to quit. She had recently begun going to cooking school at night to become a chef. This dream, she told me, felt like a reflection of her hopes and fears about the prospect of changing careers. The presence of Democratic presidential candidate Bill Clinton, a newcomer on the national political stage, embodied this theme of uncertain change. Patty is watching a group of apartment-dwelling owls (perhaps symbolizing the wisdom of her attending night school), and she suddenly finds herself sitting next to this relatively unknown political phenomenon. At first Patty doesn't recognize him, and when she finally does she still can't remember his first name. He seems to represent the future, appealing in its potential yet unknown in its actual consequences. I heard many other dreams about Bill Clinton during and after the 1992 election, several of which included similar feelings of comfort, friendliness, and intimacy with him (up to and including romantic/sexual encounters). In Patty's dream his presence has aspects of both the personal (he's a symbol of impending change in her work life) and the political (he was in fact campaigning as an agent of governmental change). The two dimensions of meaning reinforced each other, prompting Patty toward new waking-life actions—she took a new job as a cook, and she voted for Clinton in the election.

Lyndon Johnson 1: Paralysis

He began having, night after night, a terrifying dream, in which he would see himself sitting absolutely still, in a big, straight chair. In the dream, the chair stood in the middle of the great, open plains. A stampede of cattle was coming toward him. He tried to move, but he could not. He cried out again and again for his mother, but no one came.

—Doris Kearns Goodwin, *Lyndon Johnson and the American Dream* (New York: St. Martin's Griffin, 1991), 32.

Lyndon B. Johnson served as president from 1963 to 1969. He told this and the following three dream reports to former White House aide and author Doris Kearns Goodwin, whose biography of Johnson referred to the dreams as meaningful reflections of his deeper character. This one appears to be the earliest dream Johnson ever remembered, from around the age of five, and it's a horrifying image of titanic danger and existential vulnerability. Goodwin's interpretation moves in a psychoanalytic direction, treating the recurrent nightmares as symbolic indications of Johnson's oedipal attachment to his mother. His strenuous effort to deny these powerful desires, Goodwin says, gave him a lifelong fear of paralysis and a corresponding impulse toward restless action and movement. I won't dispute her references to Johnson's personal life, but I think the dreams can also be interpreted as expressions of a precocious awareness of human finitude and weakness in the face of powers vastly beyond his or anyone's ability to control. Whatever he may or may not have felt about his mother, Johnson's recurrent nightmares can be seen as reflecting the primal glimmers of mortality that have haunted the sleep of children throughout history, and that often reappear at moments of crisis later in adulthood.

Johnson told Goodwin that the paralysis dreams came back after his heart attack in 1955, when he was forty-six years old. He had just been elected majority leader of the U.S. Senate, and the months of recuperation required following the heart attack seemed to create the conditions for the titanic terrors to reappear. He said, "They [the nightmares] got worse after my heart attack. For I knew then how awful it was to lose command of myself, to be dependent on others. I couldn't stand it." This sounds like a pretty good self-analysis of the dreams, more convincing to me than the psychoanalytic approach.

Lyndon Johnson 2: Chained to His Work

In the dream, I had finished signing one stack of letters and had turned my chair toward the window. The activity on the street below suggested to me that it was just past five o'clock. All of Washington, it seemed, was on the

street, leaving work for the day, heading for home. Suddenly, I decided I'd pack up and go home, too. For once, I
decided, it would be nice to join all those people on the
street and have an early dinner with my family. I started to
get up from my chair, but I couldn't move. I looked down
at my legs and saw they were manacled to the chair with
a heavy chain. I tried to break the chain, but I couldn't. I
tried again and failed again. Once more and I gave up;
I reached for the second stack of mail. I placed it directly in
front of me, and got back to work.

—Goodwin, *Lyndon Johnson,* 167.

Johnson said this dream came in the early 1960s, when he was
serving as vice president to John F. Kennedy. It merged his recurrent paralysis nightmares with his current political dissatisfac-
tions. The vice presidency carries enormous prestige but little
actual power (until recently, at least), and Johnson's acute fear of
losing control meant he found the position frustrating in the extreme. His unhappiness with his job resonates, of course, with
the multitude of work-related nightmares discussed in previous
pages. Like many other American workers, Johnson felt trapped
in his job, cut off from his family, and too weak to escape the
greater powers that controlled his life.

Lyndon Johnson 3: The Ghost of Woodrow Wilson

[H]e was lying in a bed in the Red Room of the White
House...His head was still his, but from the neck down
his body was [a] thin, paralyzed body.

—Goodwin, *Lyndon Johnson,* 342.

This version of his recurrent dream started in 1967, when
Johnson was reaching the end of his first full term as president.

He associated the awful vision with (1) his grandmother, whose frail body frightened him as a child; and (2) Woodrow Wilson, president from 1913 to 1921, a fellow Democrat whose failures Johnson saw as emblematic of weak, impotent leadership. Wilson suffered a debilitating stroke in 1919 that effectively ended his presidency. Johnson worried about his inherited vulnerability to strokes (many in his family had died from them), and he had good reason to fear that his administration would be judged, like Wilson's, as a failure, given the worsening war in Vietnam and the terrible race riots flaring up in several American cities. His emaciating physical transformation in the dream signaled, I suspect, Johnson's growing awareness that he would soon be joining the ranks of the presidential ancestors. Goodwin says that when Johnson had these dreams he would get out of bed and walk through the White House with a small flashlight until he reached Wilson's portrait, which he would physically touch in hope of consolation, or sympathy, or perhaps forgiveness.

Lyndon Johnson 4: Swimming in Circles

In the dream he saw himself swimming in a river. He was swimming from the center toward the shore. He swam and swam, but he never seemed to get any closer. He turned around to swim to the other shore, but again he got nowhere. He was simply going round and round in circles.

—Goodwin, *Lyndon Johnson,* 344.

Johnson faced a truly paralyzing situation in 1968, the time when he reported having this dream. The Tet offensive by the North Vietnamese marked a terrible setback to the American war cause, urban racial unrest was intensifying all over the country, student protests were growing in size and passion—if Johnson tried to run for another term he would face a terrible battle against his opponents for the dubious prize of four more years of the same, and yet if he simply gave up and retreated to his home in Texas he would be roundly denounced as a coward. According to Goodwin, this new variation of his paralysis dream helped Johnson find his way beyond the either-or dilemma. He decided he would not campaign for a second term so he could better serve the country as a nonpartisan leader and peacemaker during the dangerous months ahead, before the next president took office. Goodwin says Johnson connected this dream with a story his grandfather told about cattle getting caught in river whirlpools, which I believe deepens the thematic relations with his early childhood paralysis nightmares of the thundering herd of cattle. In this dream, more than fifty years after the bad dreams first started, Johnson discovers that even the mighty cattle are vulnerable to the greater power represented by the whirlpool—just so, even the mighty president of the United States must yield to the greater power of historical forces beyond his individual ability to control. I see the image of the circles as key here. Johnson decided to devote his final years to the cause of historical continuity, carrying on the legacy of leadership from one president to the next, responsibly ending the service of his administration in order to prepare the country for the next cycle of political decision making. He stopped trying to fight against his existential weakness and chose instead to embrace the final stage of his political career as an opportunity to immerse himself wholeheartedly in the swirling currents of history.

Abraham Lincoln 1: Visitation of the Dead

Mr. Lincoln said: "Colonel, did you ever dream of a lost friend, and feel that you were holding sweet communion with that friend, and yet have a sad consciousness that it was not a reality?—just so I dream of my boy Willie."

179

Overcome with emotion, he dropped his head on the table, and sobbed aloud.

—Henry J. Raymond, *The Life of Abraham Lincoln*
(New York: Darby and Miller, 1865), 756.

Abraham Lincoln, elected president of a rapidly fragmenting country in 1860, reportedly confided this dream to in the spring of 1862 to his personal aide, Colonel Le Grand B. Cannon. Just a few months earlier Lincoln's son Willie had died at the age of eleven. Willie was the second son he and his wife, Mary, had lost (four-year-old Eddie died in 1850). Visitation dreams of deceased loved ones have been reported in many cultures around the world, reflecting the all-too-human desire to look beyond death and meet with those who have left their physical bodies. Lincoln commented on the paradoxical quality of his experience, which I've found characteristic of many visitation dreams: they are joyful *and* heartbreaking, reassuring and distressing at the same time. The vivid memorability of such dreams plays an important role in the mourning process, enabling the individual to envision a new kind of relationship with the dead person—an enduring spiritual connection of tremendous emotional power that carries over from dreaming into waking awareness. Whether you believe such dreams represent the wishful imaginings of the mind or the actual contact between a living person and a soul of the dead, visitation dreams provide people with a kind of sad wisdom that's profoundly reassuring, particularly in times of waking-life conflict and danger. That would certainly describe the situation Lincoln faced in 1862. The Civil War had begun the previous year, and he felt the unimaginable weight of personal responsibility for the country's political survival. As painful as these dreams of his dead son Willie may have been, I suspect Lincoln wouldn't have given them up for anything.

Abraham Lincoln 2: Parental Concern

Think you better put "Tad's" pistol away. I had an ugly dream about him.

> —Abraham Lincoln, *Collected Works of Abraham Lincoln* (New Brunswick: Rutgers University Press, 1953), vol. 6, note of June 9, 1863.

Lincoln sent this brief note to Mary regarding their youngest son, Tad, ten years old at the time. No details are given about this "ugly dream," and apparently no details were required. Mary would have immediately understood her husband's worry, accepted its source, and taken the necessary precautions. Lincoln's parental anxiety dream, in today's language, represented "actionable intelligence." Mary took great interest in dreams and other kinds of unusual psychospiritual phenomena, and historians have been tempted to blame her for her husband's dalliances with the supernatural. But I think we should credit Lincoln with possessing at least as much innate dreaming power as any other human, including the capacity of his nocturnal imagination to simulate realistic threats to himself and his family. The psychological potency of dreaming appears very clearly in Lincoln's brief report. The "ugly dream" provoked more awareness of a danger to one of his children, and it prompted greater vigilance in his waking life to defend against that danger.

Abraham Lincoln 3:
Who Is Dead in the White House?

About ten days ago I retired very late. I had been up waiting for important dispatches from the front. I could not have been long in bed when I fell into a slumber, for I was weary. I soon began to dream. There seemed to be a death-like stillness about me. Then I heard subdued sobs, as if a number of people were weeping. I thought I left my bed and wandered downstairs. There the silence was broken by the same pitiful sobbing, but the mourners were invisible. I went from room to room; no living person was in sight, but the same mournful sounds of distress met me as I passed along. It was light in all the rooms; every object was familiar to me; but where were all the people who were grieving as if their hearts would break? I was puzzled and alarmed. What could be the meaning of all this? Determined to find the cause of a state of things so mysterious and so shocking, I kept on until I arrived at the East Room, which I entered. There I met with a sickening surprise. Before me was a catafalque, on which rested a corpse wrapped in funeral vestments. Around it were stationed soldiers who were acting as guards; and there was a throng of people, some gazing mournfully upon the corpse, whose face was covered, others weeping pitifully. "Who is dead in the White House?" I demanded of one of the soldiers. "The President," was his answer; "he was killed by an assassin!" Then came a loud burst of grief from the crowd.

—Stephen B. Oates, *With Malice toward None: A Life of Abraham Lincoln* (New York: HarperPerennial, 1994), 425–26.

During the second week of April 1865, a few days before his assassination, Lincoln told this dream to his wife, his bodyguard Ward Hill Lamon, and one or two other people sitting with him in the White House. According to Lamon, who wrote down the conversation immediately afterward, a downcast Lincoln said the weird dream had haunted and possessed him for the past several days. Mary and Lamon both became alarmed at the ominous implications, and Lincoln tried to reassure them by saying it probably meant nothing. He doesn't seem to have believed that himself, though. Death by assassination was a real and constant threat; Lincoln knew for a fact that Southern sympathizers were eagerly plotting to kill him. He also knew from his close reading of Shakespeare and the Bible that especially memorable dreams can portend the imminence of death. His earlier night visions focused on the well-being of his children, but now his dreaming imagination turned to the dangers looming over his own life.

After Lincoln was shot the night of April 14, an anguished Mary was heard to exclaim, "His dream was prophetic!"

Abraham Lincoln 4: Victory

At the Cabinet meeting held the morning of the assassination, it was afterward remembered, a remarkable circumstance occurred. General Grant was present, and during a lull in the discussion the President turned to him and asked if he had heard from General Sherman. General Grant replied that he had not, but was in hourly expectation of receiving dispatches from him announcing the surrender of Johnston. "Well," said the President, "you will hear very soon now, and the news will be important." "Why do you think so?" said the General. "Because," said Mr. Lincoln, "I had a dream last night; and ever since the war began, I have invariably had the same dream before any important military event occurred." He then instanced Bull Run, Antietam, Gettysburg, etc., and said that before each of these events, he had had the same dream; and turning to Secretary [of the Navy] Welles, said: "It is in your line, too, Mr. Welles. The dream is, that

I saw a ship sailing very rapidly; and I am sure that it por-
tends some important national event."

—Francis Carpenter, *Six Months at the White House
with Abraham Lincoln: The Story of a Picture* (New
York: Hurd and Houghton, 1866), 292.

Here's another instance of prebattle dreaming, an apparently
frequent occurrence in Lincoln's life as military commander of
the Northern army. He had learned to associate the dreaming
image of a ship speeding across the sea with the imminent arrival
of momentous news, and on this Good Friday morning of 1865 he
felt the impulse to share his dream omens with his military com-
manders. The final triumph of the Union over the Confederacy
lay just weeks away, and Lincoln knew the war had been won.
His optimism seems tragically misplaced in light of his murder
that very night, but I'm more interested in his imparting of
oneiric wisdom to the victorious generals. In speaking so openly
about his dreams and his belief that they were legitimate sources
of warning and knowledge that helped him in his efforts to keep
the Union together, Lincoln offered his generals (including the
man who would be president from 1869 to 1877, Ulysses S.
Grant) an example of truly visionary leadership. He also offered to
the rest of American history an example of someone who relied
on his dreams to help him overcome the most serious challenges
in both his personal and collective life.

I've often heard skeptics who doubt the veracity of dream vis-
itations, prophecies, and the like—the question always remains
open whether the people reporting these marvelous experiences
are actually telling the truth or not. I can provide a detailed
philosophical response to that skeptical question when it arises,
but here I'll just boil it down to this: if you can't trust Abe Lincoln, who *can* you trust?

John Adams–Benjamin Rush 1:
Dream Sharing of the Founding Fathers

Rush set the terms for what became a high-stakes game of honesty by proposing that they dispense with the usual topics and report to each other on their respective dreams. Adams leapt at the suggestion and declared himself prepared to match his old friend "dream for dream." Rush began with a "singular dream" set in 1790 and focusing on a crazed derelict who was promising a crowd that he could "produce rain and sunshine and cause the wind to blow from any quarter he pleased." Rush interpreted this eloquent lunatic as a symbolic figure representing all those political leaders in the infant nation who claimed they could shape public opinion. Adams subsequently countered: "I dreamed that I was mounted on a lofty scaffold in the center of a great plain in Versailles, surrounded by an innumerable congregation of five and twenty millions." But the crowd was not comprised of people. Instead, they were all "inhabitants of the royal menagerie," including lions, elephants, wildcats, rats, squirrels, whales, sharks... At the end of the dream, he was forced to flee the scene with my "clothes torn from my back and my skin lacerated from head to foot."

— Joseph J. Ellis, *Founding Brothers: The Revolutionary Generation* (New York: Vintage, 2002), 214–15.

I haven't yet had the opportunity to study the original letters between John Adams and Benjamin Rush myself, so I'm relying on Ellis's reading of this remarkable correspondence (which began in 1805 and continued for many years). Adams was the country's second president (1979–1801). He played a central role in the country's revolutionary birth but found himself brusquely pushed aside by Thomas Jefferson, his erstwhile friend and compatriot, who defeated him in the 1800 election. Rush was another Founding Father, a Pennsylvania doctor who signed the Declaration of Independence and who made it his personal mission to reconcile Adams and Jefferson. He acted as an intermediary between them, writing letters to both men and trying to persuade them to restore some sense of political unity with each other, for their own sake and for the welfare of the young American republic, whose visionary system of government was still fragile and uncertain of long-term survival.

Why Rush made his dream-sharing proposal to Adams, where he got the idea, what made Adams so quickly agree—these are questions to which I don't know the answers. But it's fascinating to discover evidence that the country's earliest leaders evinced an enthusiastic willingness to share and discuss the insights revealed in their dreams. Rush's "singular" dream reflected the distaste he and Adams both felt toward the political demagoguery of their opponents, whose seductive fantasies were threatening to destroy the federal government's ability to function as originally intended. Adams responded with an elaborate nightmare (his reporting of the animals goes on for several paragraphs) in which he's overcome by the tremendous power and riotous diversity of the animal kingdom. Ellis suggests, plausibly, I think, that Adams's dream symbolized the angry emotions aroused in him by the split with Jefferson.

John Adams–Benjamin Rush 2: The End

Rush reported his most amazing dream yet. He dreamed that Adams had written a short letter to Jefferson, congratulating him on his recent retirement from public life. Jefferson had then responded to this magnanimous gesture with equivalent graciousness . . . Then the two philosopher-kings "sunk into the grave nearly at the same time, full of years and rich in the gratitude and praises of their country"... Adams responded immediately: "A DREAM AGAIN! I have no other objection to your dream but that it is not history. It may be prophecy."

—Ellis, *Founding Brothers,* 220.

In 1809, when Rush described his dream, Adams and Jefferson were still estranged. However, both men had expressed to Rush a willingness to overcome their differences and bury their hurt feelings for the higher cause of national unity. Ordinarily I would raise the skeptic's question myself—Rush's "dream" sounds too smooth, too allegorical, too conveniently supportive of his conscious goals to be believed. But as a matter of historical fact, the dream came true in a way I doubt anyone could fabricate. Adams and Jefferson resumed a cordial, respectful friendship in 1812, and for the remaining years of their lives they wrote each other detailed letters analyzing their roles in the country's founding and articulating their best understanding of the Revolution's core ideals and purposes. In uncanny obedience to Rush's dream, Adams and Jefferson died on same day—July 4, 1826, the fiftieth anniversary of the signing of the Declaration of Independence.

Appendix 2

Further Readings
in Dream Research

The notes and bibliography provide numerous references to dream-related scholarly books and articles worthy of additional study. Here I'll briefly mention what I believe are the best points of entry into the research literature.

Dreaming, sponsored by the International Association for the Study of Dreams and published by the American Psychological Association, is now in its eighteenth year as a quarterly, peer-reviewed academic journal (www.asdreams.org). It presents articles from several different disciplines, offering data from laboratory experiments, clinical case studies, literary analyses, historical investigations, and many other research methods. Anyone who's interested in learning about the latest issues, findings, and debates in the study of dreams is well advised to begin with this journal.

Another good general resource is the special series of books on dream studies published by the State University of New York Press under the general editorship of Robert L. Van de Castle. These books touch on virtually every topic in the field and include a wealth of original findings. I've found *The Functions of Dreaming,* edited by Alan Moffitt, Milton Kramer, and Robert

Hoffman; *In Search of Dreams: Results of Experimental Dream Research,* by Inge Strauch and Barbara Meier; and *Dream Reader,* by Anthony Shafton to be the most useful in my own work. I also recommend the Web site administered by G. William Domhoff, www.dreamresearch.net, which includes a library of dream research literature and an interactive archive of dozens of dream series from individuals and groups. Several of the focus group members profiled in this book agreed to include their dream series on Domhoff's site.

Readers interested in learning more about dreams in therapy and healing may consult Clara Hill's *Working with Dreams in Psychotherapy,* Rosalind Cartwright and Lynne Lamberg's *Crisis Dreaming,* Edward Bruce Bynum's *Families and the Interpretation of Dreams,* Robert Bosnak's *Tracks in the Wilderness of Dreaming,* Montague Ullman and Nan Zimmerman's *Working with Dreams,* Eugene Gendlin's *Let Your Body Interpret Your Dreams,* Alan Siegel's *Dream Wisdom,* and Jeremy Taylor's *Where People Fly and Water Runs Uphill.*

On the latest from biology, neuroscience, and cognitive psychology, I suggest turning to *Principles and Practices of Sleep Medicine,* edited by Meir H. Kryger, Thomas Roth, and William C. Dement; *Sleep and Dreaming,* edited by Ed Pace-Schott, Mark Solms, Mark Blagrove, and Steven Harnad; *Sleep and Brain Plasticity,* by Pierre Maquet, Carlyle Smith, and Robert Stickgold; *The New Science of Dreaming,* edited by Deirdre Barrett and Patrick McNamara; *Dreams and Nightmares,* by Ernest Hartmann; and *The Dream Experience,* by Milton Kramer.

Good anthropological and historical texts include Lee Irwin's *The Dream Seekers: Native American Visionary Traditions of the Great Plains,* Barbara Tedlock's edited collection *Dreaming: Anthropological and Psychological Interpretations,* Mechal Sobel's *Teach Me Dreams: The Search for Self in the Revolutionary Era,* and Carla Gerona's *Night Journeys: The Power of Dreams in Transatlantic Quaker Culture,* all of which refer in one way or another to the Americas. G. E. von Grunebaum and Roger Callois's *The Dream and Human Societies* remains my favorite source of crosscultural dream discussion.

Acknowledgments

This book would not have been possible without the generosity and persistence of the ten people who volunteered for the year of dream journaling. My gratitude goes first and foremost to them (and their patient families!). Joanne Stiller, Jennifer White, Bitsy Broughton, and Anita Sanchez helped me recruit the volunteers, conduct interviews, and sort through the data, and their professional assistance and creative insight have been vital forces in the project as a whole. At several points I relied on the guidance of particular people and groups who provided exactly the help I needed: the visitors' center of Fayetteville, North Carolina, where I received a gracious introduction to the local community; the International Association for the Study of Dreams, whose members (including Phil King, Ernest Hartmann, Stanley Krippner, Tracey Kahan, Bernard Welt, Jane White-Lewis, Sara Lev, and Lana Nasser) have offered valuable feedback since I first began this research in 1992; Tom Campbell, former U.S. representative and dean of University of California–Berkeley's Haas School of Business, who has always been generous with his advice and counsel; Jennifer Berktold and her colleagues at Greenberg Rosner Quinlan, who helped make the dream poll a reality; and Rick Polinsky, who built the perfect bonfire for an evening of political kibitzing and theological discussion. A few friends read and commented on early drafts—many thanks to Jeremy Taylor, Johanna King, Roger Knudson, Bill Domhoff, and Rita Dwyer. Amy Caldwell has been a stellar editorial guide from the very beginning. I appreciate her support and that of the whole Beacon Press staff.

Most important, I've been blessed with an extended family of well-informed and highly opinionated individuals who throw themselves into political debates at the slightest provocation. My deepest thanks go to Hilary, Ned, Tish, Howard, Marie C., Jim, Jean, Sharon, Marie B., Bob, Michelle, Kevin, Alex, and Kim, my personal cadre of provocative pundits.

Notes

Introduction

1. The group of ten people never met as a whole, so they don't fit the strict definition of a focus group. I am using the term in a broader sense, referring to a small number of people whose opinions and experiences are subjected to detailed, systematic, contemporaneous study.

2. A further methodological disclosure: the ten participants were not paid for keeping the journals, though I did make a monetary donation in their name to the charity of their choice. At the outset I explained to them the nature of my project, described the distressing emotions that might arise from remembering dreams, and reassured them they could withdraw from the project at any time and consult with a mental health professional if they so desired. As it turned out, no one reported any problems caused by the journal-keeping process. On the contrary, every one of them described it as enjoyable and personally enlightening. My interest in their dreams undoubtedly affected the content of their reports, but I had little contact with them during the journaling year in order to create the best conditions for their natural dream patterns to emerge and be recorded. I believe the major effect of my influence

on their dreaming was quantitative, not qualitative. The participants definitely remembered more dreams than usual during that year, but the basic themes, images, and motifs of the dreams seemed to be consistent with their past experiences.

3. Adams, *The Epic of America,* 404.

1. Conservatives and Liberals, Awake and Asleep

1. Safire, *Safire's New Political Dictionary.* For more on current research in political psychology, see Sears, Huddy, and Jervis, *Oxford Handbook of Political Psychology* and Jost and Sidanius, *Political Psychology.* The International Society for Political Psychology also provides top-quality resources in this field (www.ispp.org).

2. American political demographics: "Special Report: America at 300 Million: The United Stats of America," *Time Magazine,* October 30, 2006. Younger Americans trending liberal: "Young Americans Are Leaning Left, New Poll Finds," *New York Times,* June 27, 2007; "Poll Shows GOP Losing Ground with Youth," *San Francisco Chronicle,* August 27, 2007.

3. The science of sleep: Carskadon, *Encyclopedia of Sleep and Dreaming;* Dement and Vaughn, *The Promise of Sleep;* Kryger, Roth, and Dement, *Principles and Practices of Sleep Medicine.*

4. See Killgore et. al, "The Effects of 53 Hours of Sleep Deprivation on Moral Judgment"; Harrison and Horne, "One Night of Sleep Loss Impairs Innovative Thinking and Flexible Decision Making"; Rechtschaffen et al., "Physiological Correlates of Prolonged Sleep Deprivation in Rats."

5. I discuss this at greater length in *Dreaming in the World's Religions.*

6. For a review and discussion of this literature, see Pace-Schott et al., *Sleep and Dreaming;* Barrett and McNamara, *The New Science of Dreaming.*

7. See Domhoff, *Finding Meaning in Dreams* and *The Scientific Study of Dreams;* Hall, "Diagnosing Personality by the Analysis of Dreams."

8. Schredl, "Dream Recall."

9. Conception dreams: Bulkeley, "The Origins of Dreaming."

10. Jung, "On the Nature of Dreams," 36. See also Rebecca Cathcart,

"Winding through 'Big Dreams' Are the Threads of Our Lives," *New York Times*, July 3, 2007.

11. Domhoff, "An Unsuccessful Search for Further Correlates of Everyday Dream Recall"; Kroth et al., "Incidence of Having Dreamed and Conservative Political Attitudes."

12. Bulkeley, "Political Dreaming: Dreams of the 1992 Presidential Election."

13. Bulkeley, "Dream Content and Political Ideology."

14. These comments came in response to questions posed by Associated Press reporter Mike Martin.

15. Bulkeley, "Sleep and Dream Patterns of Political Liberals and Conservatives."

16. Because of rounding to whole numbers, some columns do not add up to 100 percent. My friends in the social sciences have pointed out the many uncertainties that bedevil the use of simple statistics like these in arguing for broad psychological theories. I share their concerns, which were well expressed by Tocqueville: "When statistical method is not based upon rigorously accurate calculations, it leads to error rather than to guidance. The mind easily allows itself to be deluded by the deceptive appearance of precision which statistics retain even when wrong and it relies confidently upon mistakes apparently clothed in the forms of mathematical truth" (*Democracy in America*, 255). I fully recognize the limits of these data, but I'll stand by the rigor and accuracy of my calculations regarding the sleep and dream patterns of contemporary Americans until other researchers come up with something better.

17. Lauderdale et al., "Objectively Measured Sleep Characteristics among Early-Middle-Aged Adults."

2. The War on Terror

1. Hartmann and Basile, "Dream Imagery Becomes More Intense After 9/11/01."

2. I have not seen the dream reports gathered by Hartmann and Basile, so I cannot directly compare the frequency of incorporation dreams in their data set and ours.

3. Pace-Schott et al., *Sleep and Dreaming;* Solms, *The Neuropsychology of Dreams;* Fosse and Domhoff, "Dreaming as Non-executive Orienting."

4. Allan Hobson, *Dreaming as Delirium,* 117.

5. Siegel, *Dream Wisdom;* Bynum, *Families and the Interpretation of Dreams.*

6. Cartwright and Lamberg, *Crisis Dreaming,* 269.

7. Foulkes, *Children's Dreaming and the Development of Consciousness;* Domhoff, *Finding Meaning in Dreams.*

8. Revonsuo, "The Reinterpretation of Dreams," also found in Pace-Schott et al., *Sleep and Dreaming;* Valli and Revonsuo, "Evolutionary Psychological Approaches to Dream Content."

9. Taylor, *Dream Work;* Sullivan, *Recurring Dreams;* Domhoff, *Finding Meaning in Dreams* and *The Scientific Study of Dreams.*

10. Solms, *The Neuropsychology of Dreams;* Braun et al., "Regional Cerebral Blood Flow throughout the Sleep-Wake Cycle"; Maquet et al., "Functional Neuroanatomy of Human Rapid-Eye-Movement Sleep and Dreaming"; Nofzinger et al., "Forebrain Activation in REM Sleep."

11. Van de Castle, *Our Dreaming Mind,* 24. For another example of this kind of dream from President Abraham Lincoln, see appendix 1.

12. Hobson and McCarley, "The Brain as a Dream State Generator"; Crick and Mitchison, "The Function of Dream Sleep."

13. Hunt, *The Multiplicity of Dreams;* Hartmann, *Dreams and Nightmares;* Jung, "On the Nature of Dreams."

3. Religion, Spirituality, and Faith

1. "Special Report: America at 300 Million."

2. Gallup poll, May 10–13, 2007.

3. Green, "Religion Gap Swings New Ways," 3.

4. Silk and Green, "The GOP's Religion Problem."

5. Von Grunebaum and Callois, *The Dream in Human Societies;* Young, *Dreaming in the Lotus;* Tedlock, *Dreaming;* Szpakowska, *Behind Closed Eyes;* Shulman and Stroumsa, eds., *Dream Cultures;*

O'Flaherty, *Dreams, Illusion, and Other Realities;* Lohmann, *Dream Travelers;* Jedrej and Shaw, *Dreaming, Religion, and Society in Africa;* Irwin, *The Dream Seekers.*

6. Bulkeley, "The Origins of Dreaming."
7. Maybruck, *Pregnancy and Dreams.*
8. *Time* poll: "Survey on Faith and the Presidential Election," May 10–13, 2007.
9. Current efforts to counter that tendency are led by Unitarian Universalist minister Jeremy Taylor, Episcopalian minister Bob Haden, and Presbyterian minister Geoff Nelson.

4. The Natural Environment

1. See, for example, the *Los Angeles Times*/Bloomberg poll published August 4, 2006: 73 percent of the country regard global warming as a serious problem; 78 percent think the government should do more to limit carbon dioxide emissions; 56 percent think the Bush administration is not doing enough to protect the environment.
2. The second annual "America's Report Card on the Environment" survey, by the Woods Institute for the Environment at Stanford University in collaboration with the Associated Press, September 25, 2007.
3. Tocqueville, *Democracy in America,* 562–63.
4. Good historical sources on America's relationship with nature include Nash, *Wilderness and the American Mind* and Albanese, *Nature Religion in America.*
5. Emerson, *Selected Writings,* 189.
6. Summarized in Domhoff, *Finding Meaning in Dreams* and Van de Castle, *Our Dreaming Mind.* See also Strauch and Meier, *In Search of Dreams;* Hillman, *Dream Animals.*
7. Strauch and Meier, based on the analysis of five hundred REM dreams, found animals in 10 percent of them (*In Search of Dreams,* 110). This figure corresponds to the 9.5 percent of dreams with at least one animal in the Hall and Van de Castle norm dreams (see www.dreambank.net).

8. Kip pointed out to me the irony of her being liberal and working with domesticated animals, while Richard the conservative works with wild animals.

9. See Harvey, *Shamanism;* Hayden, *Shamans, Sorcerers, and Saints;* Lewis-Williams, *The Mind in the Cave;* Tedlock, *The Woman in the Shaman's Body.*

5. Work and Money

1. Adams, *The Epic of America,* 404.
2. One night Nadine made no entry regarding her sleep quality.
3. Bulkeley, "Sleep and Dream Patterns of Political Liberals and Conservatives."
4. Solms, *The Neuropsychology of Dreams;* Hartmann, "We Do Not Dream of the Three R's."
5. For example, see Liebow, *Tell Them Who I Am.*

6. Family Values

1. Bulkeley, "Sleep and Dream Patterns of Political Liberals and Conservatives."
2. A deeper analysis of Lola's dream would go on to explore the symbolic dimensions of bridges in culture, myth, art, and religion. Once again, I don't want to suggest that my interpretations rule out other possible meanings in the dreams. On the contrary, I believe every dream has multiple layers of significance, the most important of which often do not emerge quickly or easily. My approach in this book basically goes for the low-hanging fruit. I'm trying to provide a relatively simple and straightforward means of entry into *some* of the meanings in these dreams, which I hope will encourage readers to explore further realms of dream meaning according to their own intuitive insights.

Conclusion

1. Alford, Funk, and Hibbing, "Are Political Orientations Genetically Transmitted?" Westen, *The Political Brain;* Jennings and Niemi, *Generations and Politics.* A good review of this literature is

in Erin O'Donnell, "Twigs Bent Left or Right: Understanding How Liberals and Conservatives Differ, from Conception On," *Harvard Magazine,* January–February 2006, 34–39.

2. For example, see the Washington Post/ABC News Poll released May 16, 2006, reporting 69 percent of the American public saying the country is on the wrong track; "The American Dream Survey 2006," conducted by Lake Research Partners, showing that 80 percent of working Americans believe the country's financial burdens will increase in the next ten years; "Metlife Study of the American Dream 2007," conducted by Strategy First Partners/Penn, Schoen, and Berland Associates, shows only 18 percent of the American public believing the next generation of Americans will be better off economically than the current generation, and 51 percent believing the next generation will be worse off.

3. Jost et al., "Political Conservatism as Motivated Social Cognition," 339.

4. Adorno et al., *The Authoritarian Personality.* The notion of psychological boundaries comes from Hartmann, *Boundaries in the Mind.* See also Rokeach, *The Open and Closed Mind.*

5. Lakoff and Johnson, *Metaphors We Live By;* Lakoff, "How Metaphor Structures Dreams."

6. Lakoff, *Moral Politics.*

7. Samuels, *The Political Psyche,* 3–4.

8. Niebuhr, *Moral Man and Immoral Society,* 81.

Bibliography

Adams, James Truslow. *The Epic of America*. Boston: Little, Brown, 1931.

Adorno, T. W., E. Frenkel-Brunswick, D. J. Levinson, and R. N. Sanford. *The Authoritarian Personality*. New York: Harper, 1950.

Albanese, Catherine L. *Nature Religion in America: From the Algonkian Indians to the New Age*. Chicago: University of Chicago Press, 1990.

Alford, John R., Carolyn L. Funk, and John R. Hibbing. "Are Political Orientations Genetically Transmitted?" *American Political Science Review* 99, no. 2 (2005): 153–67.

Barrett, Deirdre, and Patrick McNamara, eds. *The New Science of Dreaming*. 3 vols. Westport, CT: Praeger, 2007.

Bosnak, Robert. *Tracks in the Wilderness of Dreaming: Exploring Interior Landscape through Practical Dreamwork*. New York: Delacorte, 1996.

Braun, A. R., T. J. Balkin, N. J. Wesensten, R. E. Carson, M. Varga, P. Baldwin, S. Selbie, G. Belenky, and P. Herscovitch. "Regional Cerebral Blood Flow throughout the Sleep-Wake Cycle." *Brain* 120 (1997): 1173–97.

Bulkeley, Kelly. "Dream Content and Political Ideology." *Dreaming* 12, no. 2 (2002): 61–78.

Bibliography

————. *Dreaming in the World's Religions: A Comparative History.* New York: New York University Press, 2008.

————."The Origins of Dreaming." In *Where God and Science Meet,* edited by P. McNamara. Westport, CT: Praeger, 2006.

————. "Political Dreaming: Dreams and the 1992 Presidential Election." In *Among All These Dreamers: Essays on Dreams and Modern Society,* edited by K. Bulkeley. Albany: State University of New York Press, 1996.

————. "Sleep and Dream Patterns of Political Liberals and Conservatives." *Dreaming* 16, no. 3 (2006): 223–35.

Bynum, Edward Bruce. *Families and the Interpretation of Dreams: Awakening the Intimate Web.* New York: Harrington Park, 1993.

Carskadon, Mary A., ed. *Encyclopedia of Sleep and Dreaming.* New York: Macmillan, 1993.

Cartwright, Rosalind, and Lynne Lamberg. *Crisis Dreaming.* New York: Harper Collins, 1992.

Crick, Francis, and Graeme Mitchison. "The Function of Dream Sleep." *Nature* 304 (1983): 111–14.

Dement, William C., and Christopher Vaughn. *The Promise of Sleep.* New York: Dell, 1999.

Domhoff, G. William. *Finding Meaning in Dreams: A Quantitative Approach.* New York: Plenum, 1996.

————. *The Scientific Study of Dreams: Neural Networks, Cognitive Development, and Content Analysis.* Washington, DC: American Psychological Association, 2003.

————. "An Unsuccessful Search for Further Correlates of Everyday Dream Recall." *Psychophysiology* 4, no. 3 (1968): 386.

Emerson, Ralph Waldo. *Selected Writings of Ralph Waldo Emerson.* New York: Signet Classic, 1965.

Flanagan, Owen. *Dreaming Souls: Sleep, Dreams, and the Evolution of the Conscious Mind.* Oxford: Oxford University Press, 2000.

Fosse, Roar, and G. William Domhoff. "Dreaming as Non-executive Orienting: A Conceptual Framework for Consciousness during

Sleep." In *The New Science of Dreaming,* edited by Deirdre Barrett and Patrick McNamara. Westport, CT: Praeger, 2007.

Foulkes, David. *Children's Dreaming and the Development of Consciousness.* Cambridge, MA: Harvard University Press, 1999.

Freud, Sigmund. *The Interpretation of Dreams.* Translated by James Strachey. New York: Avon, 1965.

Gendlin, Eugene. *Let Your Body Interpret Your Dreams.* Wilmette, IL: Chiron, 1985.

Gerona, Carla. *Night Journeys: The Power of Dreams in Transatlantic Quaker Culture.* Charlottesville: University of Virginia Press, 2004.

Green, John C. "Religion Gap Swings New Ways." *Religion in the News* 7 (2005): 2–3.

Hall, Calvin. "Diagnosing Personality by the Analysis of Dreams." *Journal of Abnormal and Social Psychology* 42 (1947): 68–79.

Harrison, Y., and J. A. Horne. "One Night of Sleep Loss Impairs Innovative Thinking and Flexible Decision Making." *Organizational Behavior and Human Decision Making Processes* 78, no. 2 (1999): 128–45.

Hartmann, Ernest. *Boundaries in the Mind: A New Psychology of Personality.* New York: Basic, 1993.

———. *Dreams and Nightmares: The New Theory on the Origin and Meaning of Dreams.* New York: Plenum, 1998.

———. "We Do Not Dream of the Three R's: Implications for the Nature of Dreaming Mentation." *Dreaming* 10, no. 2 (2000): 103–10.

Hartmann, Ernest, and Robert Basile. "Dream Imagery Becomes More Intense After 9/11/01." *Dreaming* 13, no. 2 (2003): 61–66.

Harvey, Graham, ed. *Shamanism: A Reader.* London: Routledge, 2003.

Hayden, Brian. *Shamans, Sorcerers, and Saints: A Prehistory of Religion.* Washington, DC: Smithsonian, 2003.

Hill, Clara. *Working with Dreams in Psychotherapy.* New York: Guilford, 2004.

Hillman, James. *Dream Animals.* San Francisco: Chronicle, 1997.

Hobson, J. Allan. *Dreaming as Delirium: How the Brain Goes Out of Its Mind.* Cambridge, MA: MIT Press, 1999.

Bibliography

Hobson, J. Allan, and Robert McCarley. "The Brain as a Dream State Generator: An Activation-Synthesis Hypothesis of the Dream Process." *American Journal of Psychiatry* 134 (1977): 1335–48.

Hunt, Harry. *The Multiplicity of Dreams: Memory, Imagination, and Consciousness.* New Haven: Yale University Press, 1989.

Irwin, Lee. *The Dream Seekers: Native American Visionary Traditions of the Great Plains.* Norman: University of Oklahoma Press, 1994.

———. *Visionary Worlds: The Making and Unmaking of Reality.* Albany: State University of New York Press, 1996.

Jedrej, M. C., and Rosalind Shaw, eds. *Dreaming, Religion, and Society in Africa.* Leiden: E. J. Brill, 1992.

Jennings, M. Kentand, and Richard G. Niemi. *Generations and Politics.* Princeton: Princeton University Press, 1981.

Jost, J. T., J. Glaser, A. W. Kruglanski, and F. J. Sulloway. "Political Conservativism as Motivated Social Cognition." *Psychological Bulletin* 129 (2003): 339–75.

Jost, J. T., and Jim Sidanius, eds. *Political Psychology: Key Readings.* New York: Psychology, 2004.

Jung, C. G. "On the Nature of Dreams." In *Dreams.* Princeton: Princeton University Press, 1974. Original edition, 1948.

Killgore, William D. S., Desiree B. Killgore, Lisa M. Day, Christopher Li, Gary H. Kamimori, and Thomas J. Balkin. "The Effects of 53 Hours of Sleep Deprivation on Moral Judgment." *Sleep* 30, no. 3 (2007): 345–52.

Kramer, Milton. *The Dream Experience: A Systematic Exploration.* New York: Routledge, 2007.

Kroth, Jerry, Christine Bautista, Joy Bess, Kristen Cruickshank, and Janet Stashak. "Incidence of Having Dreamed and Conservative Political Attitudes." *Psychological Reports* 98 (2006): 923–26.

Kryger, Meir H., Thomas Roth, and William C. Dement, eds. *Principles and Practices of Sleep Medicine.* 4th ed. Philadelphia: Elsevier Saunders, 2005.

Lakoff, George. "How Metaphor Structures Dreams: The Theory of

Conceptual Metaphor Applied to Dream Analysis." In *Dreams: A Reader on the Religious, Cultural, and Psychological Dimensions of Dreaming,* edited by Kelly Bulkeley. New York: Palgrave, 2001.

———. *Moral Politics: What Conservatives Know that Liberals Don't.* Chicago: University of Chicago Press, 1996.

Lakoff, George, and Mark Johnson. *Metaphors We Live By.* Chicago: University of Chicago Press, 1980.

Lauderdale, Diane S., Kristen L. Knutson, Lijing L. Yan, Paul J. Rathouz, Stephen B. Hulley, Steve Sidney, and Kiang Liu. "Objectively Measured Sleep Characteristics among Early-Middle-Aged Adults." *American Journal of Epidemiology* 164, no. 1 (2006): 5–16.

Lewis-Williams, David. *The Mind in the Cave.* London: Thames and Hudson, 2002.

Liebow, Elliot. *Tell Them Who I Am: The Lives of Homeless Women.* New York: Penguin, 1995.

Lohmann, Roger, ed. *Dream Travelers: Sleep Experiences and Culture in the South Pacific.* New York: Palgrave Macmillan, 2003.

Maquet, P., J. M. Peteres, J. Aerts, G. Delfiore, C. Degueldre, A. Luxen, and G. Franck. "Functional Neuroanatomy of Human Rapid-Eye-Movement Sleep and Dreaming." *Nature* 383 (1996): 163.

Maquet, Pierre, Carlyle Smith, and Robert Stickgold, eds. *Sleep and Brain Plasticity.* Oxford: Oxford University Press, 2003.

Maybruck, Patricia. *Pregnancy and Dreams.* Los Angeles: Jeremy P. Tarcher, 1989.

Moffitt, Alan, Milton Kramer, and Robert Hoffman, eds. *The Functions of Dreaming.* Albany: State University of New York Press, 1993.

Nash, Roderick. *Wilderness and the American Mind.* New Haven: Yale University Press, 1967.

Niebuhr, Reinhold. *Moral Man and Immoral Society: A Study in Ethics and Politics.* New York: Scribners, 1960.

Nofzinger, E. A., M. A. Mintun, M. B. Wiseman, D. J. Kupfer, and R. Y. Moore. "Forebrain Activation in REM Sleep: An FDG PET Study." *Brain Research* 770 (1997): 192–201.

O'Flaherty, Wendy Doniger. *Dreams, Illusion, and Other Realities.* Chicago: University of Chicago Press. 1984.

Pace-Schott, Ed, Mark Solms, Mark Blagrove, and Steven Harnad, eds. *Sleep and Dreaming: Scientific Advances and Reconsiderations.* Cambridge: Cambridge University Press, 2003.

Rechtschaffen, A., M. A. Gilliland, B. M. Bermann, and J. B. Winter. "Physiological Correlates of Prolonged Sleep Deprivation in Rats." *Science* 221, no. 4606 (1983): 182–84.

Revonsuo, Antti. "The Reinterpretation of Dreams: An Evolutionary Hypothesis of the Function of Dreaming." *Behavioral and Brain Sciences* 23, no. 6 (2000): 877–901.

Rokeach, Milton. *The Open and Closed Mind.* New York: Basic, 1960.

Safire, William. *Safire's New Political Dictionary.* New York: Random House, 1993.

Samuels, Andrew. *The Political Psyche.* London: Routledge, 1993.

Schredl, Michael. "Dream Recall: Models and Empirical Data." In *The New Science of Dreaming,* edited by Deirdre Barrett and Patrick McNamara. Westport, CT: Praeger, 2007.

Sears, David O., Leonie Huddy, and Robert Jervis, eds. *Oxford Handbook of Political Psychology.* Oxford: Oxford University Press, 2003.

Shafton, Anthony. *Dream Reader.* Albany: State University of New York Press, 1995.

Shulman, David, and David Stroumsa, eds. *Dream Cultures: Explorations in the Comparative History of Dreaming.* New York: Oxford University Press, 1999.

Siegel, Alan. *Dream Wisdom: Uncovering Life's Answers in Your Dreams.* Berkeley: Celestial Arts, 2003.

Silk, Mark, and John C. Green. "The GOP's Religion Problem." *Religion in the News* 8 (2007): 2–4.

Sobel, Mechal. *Teach Me Dreams: The Search for Self in the Revolutionary Era.* Princeton: Princeton University Press, 2000.

Solms, Mark. *The Neuropsychology of Dreams: A Clinico-Anatomical Study.* Mahwah, NJ: Lawrence Erlbaum, 1997.

Bibliography

Strauch, Inge, and Barbara Meier. *In Search of Dreams: Results of Experimental Dream Research.* Albany: State University of New York Press, 1996.

Sullivan, Kathleen. *Recurring Dreams: A Journey to Wholeness.* Freedom, CA: Crossing, 1998.

Szpakowska, Kasia. *Behind Closed Eyes: Dreams and Nightmares in Ancient Egypt.* Swansea: Classical Press of Wales, 2003.

Taylor, Jeremy. *Dream Work: Techniques for Discovering the Creative Power in Dreams.* Mahwah, NJ: Paulist, 1983.

———. *Where People Fly and Water Runs Uphill.* New York: Warner, 1992.

Tedlock, Barbara, ed. *Dreaming: Anthropological and Psychological Interpretations.* New York: Cambridge University Press, 1987.

———. *The Woman in the Shaman's Body: Reclaiming the Feminine in Religion and Medicine.* New York: Bantam, 2005.

Tocqueville, Alexis de. *Democracy in America.* Translated by G. E. Bevan. New York: Penguin, 2003.

Ullman, Montague, and Nan Zimmerman. *Working with Dreams.* Los Angeles: Jeremy P. Tarcher, 1979.

Valli, Katja, and Antti Revonsuo. 2007. "Evolutionary Psychological Approaches to Dream Content." In *The New Science of Dreaming,* edited by D. Barrett and P. McNamara. Westport, CT: Praeger.

Van de Castle, Robert. *Our Dreaming Mind.* New York: Ballantine, 1994.

Von Grunebaum, G. E., and Roger Callois, eds. *The Dream and Human Societies.* Berkeley: University of California Press, 1966.

Westen, Drew. *The Political Brain: The Role of Emotion in Deciding the Fate of the Nation.* New York: PublicAffairs, 2007.

Young, Serinity. *Dreaming in the Lotus: Buddhist Dream Narrative, Imagery, and Practice.* Boston: Wisdom, 1999.

Index

Index